794

Twayne's United States Authors Series

Sylvia E. Bowman, *Editor*

INDIANA UNIVERSITY

Willa Cather

TUSAS 258

Willa Cather

WILLA CATHER

By PHILIP GERBER

State University of New York, Brockport

TWAYNE PUBLISHERS
A DIVISION OF G. K. HALL & CO., BOSTON

Library of Congress Cataloging in Publication Data

Gerber, Philip L
  Willa Cather.

  (Twayne's United States authors series; 258)
  Bibliography: pp. 174–79.
  Includes index.
    1.   Cather, Willa Sibert, 1873–1947—Criticism and
interpretation.
PS3505.A87Z645   813'.5'2   75-2287
ISBN 0-8057-7155-7

FOR ARTHUR AND LEORA HAYES

Contents

About the Author

Philip L. Gerber has taught American literature at universities in Texas, Utah, California, and South Dakota. He is currently Professor of English on the Brockport campus of the State University of New York, and also holds the rank of Faculty Exchange Professor within the SUNY system. He has published articles on a variety of modern figures including Theodore Dreiser, William Carlos Williams, Amy Lowell, Robert Frost, and Harriet Monroe; two of his books, *Theodore Dreiser* and *Robert Frost*, have appeared in Twayne's United States Authors Series.

Preface

Dorothy Canfield Fisher, who had known Willa Cather since they were fellow students at the University of Nebraska in the 1890s, commented in 1933 upon the widely held impression of "disconnectedness" in Cather's writing; for instance, that a novel such as *A Lost Lady* had little in common with *Shadows on the Rock*. Mrs. Fisher argued that, on the contrary, all of Cather's novels were cut from the same cloth and that, whatever their differences, both novels cited were but two treatments of the same theme. While my own conclusions are not identical to hers, I agree with Mrs. Fisher's emphasis upon the unity of Cather's novels and stories.

The findings reached in this study may be attributed in part to the vast number of Cather studies made available in the forty years, since Mrs. Fisher wrote. When I worked at my dissertation on Cather five years after the author's death, the only substantial critical studies at hand were the early assessment by René Rapin and the slim critical introduction by David Daiches, both of them valuable and yet both also limited by the writers' being non-American, while Cather is above all an American product. In those pre-Xerox times the dozens of stories that Cather had published and left to perish were to be found only by a diligent search of musty periodical files, and her journalism of two decades was not only unavailable but for the most part unknown and unidentified.

Since then, of course, not only has the crucial Brown-Edel biography appeared, but a series of remarkable memoirs by long-time friends has helped to shift attention toward the hitherto closed book of Cather's early years and career. The first major step in this direction was the publication in 1951 of Mildred R. Bennett's *The World of Willa Cather.* The novelist had come to national attention between 1915 and 1920, a period in which T. K. Whipple described her achievement as a triumph of mind over Nebraska; and the tendency for a good while was to consider her an instant genius sprung full-blown upon the literary scene, much as if one hand had relinquished the reins of the pony on which she galloped over the windy plains while the other had taken up a pen and begun composing masterpieces. Mrs. Bennett's study served notice that any serious Cather student must consider a long foreground, those years before Cather reached the age of forty and made her initial venture into the novel. In the past two decades, chiefly from the University of Nebraska, has poured a flood of materials that, taken together, provide access to early publications indicating that Cather's popularly known works constitute only the most public portion of a much larger and more diverse output.

New investigations into Willa Cather's early career confirm Fanny Butcher's awareness of her friend as the most completely fulfilled person she ever knew—"fulfilled" in this case meaning Cather's winning not fame and fortune but the freedom to devote herself to the one thing she wanted most in the world to do, to write. Willa Cather's ambition was to become a perfect artist. To this end her life was dedicated, and at the height of her reputation she was hailed as having fully achieved her aim. This acclaim was not fortuitous; its foundations were laid decades before the event. For rather than being disconnected, Cather's works flow from one book to another, from one stage of development to the next, with a logic that is impressive if not unique. Her development both as theorist and as practitioner was consistent, and her mature works owe much to preliminary attempts made long before. We can demonstrate that, for instance, *The Professor's House* (1925) has its origins in a short story published in 1902 and that the principles articulated in "The Novel Démeublé" (1922) are a distillation of ideas arrived at via theatrical-literary reviews dating from the 1890s.

A major aim of this study is to indicate something of this development. I have approached the novels thematically, finding in them a singleness of thought always connected intimately with the author's own life and effort and expressing itself in two directions:

one turns inward upon the individual spirit; the other, outward with a concern for the American nation. The novels are the pièces de résistance in any study of Willa Cather, of course, and most attention is paid to them. I have also taken into account those shorter works whose study will enhance our understanding and appreciation of the novels, and I have attempted to provide a helpful discussion of Cather the literary theorist, not only for its close link with her practice of the writing art but for its intrinsic value to students of literature.

PHILIP L. GERBER

State University of New York
Brockport

Acknowledgments

Because Willa Cather and her writing have been a continuing interest for me over a long period of time, it is not an easy task to acknowledge all those whose influence and direct aid may have helped in producing the present study; yet the following should be named:

The late Professor Bartholow V. Crawford of the University of Iowa directed the dissertation that was my first attempt at expressing the enduring values of Cather's fiction. His encouragement and many kindnesses are good memories.

Mildred R. Bennett, of the Willa Cather Pioneer Memorial in Red Cloud, Nebraska, generously furnished access to Memorial holdings, including Cather letters such as those to the friend of her girlhood, Carrie Miner Sherwood. During my visit to Red Cloud Mrs. Bennett arranged that I should meet Mrs. Sherwood, then in her nineties, a rare treat; she also served as a personal guide to landmarks of the "Catherland" area surrounding Red Cloud, an invaluable aid in comprehending the status of "place" in Cather's work.

At an early stage of this study, the University of South Dakota provided research funds that enabled me to obtain essential materials and also to visit locations used in the various Cather novels, including Red Cloud. At a later stage the State University of New York provided a leave of absence that furnished the blocks of undisturbed time that ease the composition process.

While I was completing my work, Bernice Slote considerately invited me to attend the Willa Cather International Seminar, held at the University of Nebraska in observance of the author's centennial. To be immersed at a critical moment in a sea of Cather relatives, friends, publishers, and scholars and to hear their reminiscences and opinions publically expounded as well as privately communicated were unexpected pleasures. More, it gave me an unparalleled opportunity both to crystallize and to correct my thinking.

To the Newberry Library and to the Alderman Library of the University of Virginia I am indebted for primary materials. In Charlottesville Michael Plunkett furnished access to Willa Cather's correspondence and, in many instances, furnished copies of letters; Edmund Berkeley, Jr., generously granted permission to reproduce a Cather photograph.

Finally, as twice before, I owe Sylvia Bowman a gesture of appreciation for her close reading of the manuscript, for her astute corrections in both style and substance, and for her intelligent suggestions toward improving the book as a whole.

Chronology

1873   Willa Cather, born December 7 in Back Creek Valley, west of Winchester, Virginia.

1883   Moves with family to Webster County, Nebraska; resides at Catherton.

1884   Moves with family to Red Cloud, Nebraska.

1890   Graduates from high school; enters University of Nebraska, Lincoln.

1893   Begins writing dramatic criticism for *Nebraska State Journal*, Lincoln.

1895   Graduates from University of Nebraska; resides in Red Cloud and Lincoln.

1896   Moves in June to Pittsburgh as editor for *Home Monthly*.

1897   Summer residence in Nebraska; returns to Pittsburgh and post on *Pittsburgh Leader*.

1900– First meeting with Isabelle McClung; winter of free-lance
1901   writing in Washington, D. C.; returns to Pittsburgh.

1901– Teaches Latin and English at Central High School,
1903   Pittsburgh; summer in Europe (1902) with Isabelle McClung.

1903– Teaches English at Allegheny High School; *April Twilights*
1906   (1903); *The Troll Garden* (1905).

1906– Joins *McClure's* in New York City (May); research trip to
1912   Boston (1907–08) for *McClure's;* first meetings with Mrs. James T. Fields and Sarah Orne Jewett; fall 1911 resides in Cherry Valley, New York; composes "Alexandra" and "The Bohemian Girl" (stories) and completes *Alexander's Bridge* (novel); leaves *McClure's*.

1912   Publishes *Alexander's Bridge* and "The Bohemian Girl"; visits Arizona; first contact with cliff-dweller civilization.

1913	Publishes *O Pioneers!*; meets Olive Fremstad, model for Thea Kronborg; composes *The Song of the Lark*.
1914–1915	Resides in Pittsburgh; completes *The Song of the Lark*.
1915	Publishes *The Song of the Lark*; visits Mesa Verde and Taos.
1918	Publishes *My Ántonia*.
1920	Begins association with Alfred A. Knopf; publishes *Youth and the Bright Medusa*.
1922	Publishes *One of Ours*.
1923	*One of Ours* awarded Pulitzer Prize for 1922; publishes *A Lost Lady*.
1925	Publishes *The Professor's House*; edits the short stories of Sarah Orne Jewett; summer residence in New Mexico.
1926	Publishes *My Mortal Enemy*; provides introduction for Stephen Crane's *Wounds in the Rain*; summer residence in New Mexico *re* composition of *Death Comes for the Archbishop*.
1927	Publishes *Death Comes for the Archbishop*.
1928	Visits Quebec; begins *Shadows on the Rock*.
1930	Awarded Howells medal for fiction by the Academy of the National Institute of Arts and Letters.
1931	Publishes *Shadows on the Rock*.
1932	Publishes *Obscure Destinies*.
1933	Awarded Prix Fémina Américain for *Shadows on the Rock*.
1935	Publishes *Lucy Gayheart*.
1936	Publishes *Not Under Forty*.
1937–1938	The Library Edition of Cather's collected works published by Houghton Mifflin.
1940	Publishes *Sapphira and the Slave Girl*.
1944	Awarded gold medal of the National Institute of Arts and Letters.
1947	Dies, April 24, in New York City.
1948	Posthumous publication of *The Old Beauty and Others*.
1949	Posthumous publication of *Willa Cather on Writing*.

CHAPTER 1

From the World to Nebraska

> The old West, the old time,
> The old wind singing through
> The red, red grass a thousand miles . . .
> —Willa Cather, 1903

ON a day in March 1883 the Burlington Railroad deposited a Virginia family at its little station a mile from the settlement of Red Cloud, Nebraska. The group included, besides the parents and four young children, a grandmother, two cousins who had decided to join the adventure, and a hired girl and her brother. This was the Charles Cather party, which had come at the end of a long journey to strange, unfamiliar land. The detrainment was a momentous one, for it introduced to this yet untamed country the family's nine-year-old daughter Willa, who later described it as both her happiness and her curse and who produced from her encounter with it the novels that won her an enduring place in American literary history.

I *On the Gulf Stream of Migration*

In the decade following the Civil-War shock to the American populace, the westering fever that struck Willa Cather's family rose to epidemic level. The cry "Go West!" came as an answer to frustration and hard times for Southerners. Beyond the Missouri lay empty miles of cheap land where one was free to lose himself, if he wished, or to cling near the scattered settlements. This impulse opened a door, and the railroads proposed to carry one and all through it into a new American Eden.

In Nebraska the Burlington and Missouri River Railroad, awarded immense tracts as an incentive to laying rails into new territory, took the lead. Buyers in quantity seemed to wait only for the access to the land the Burlington aimed at providing. Its mission was to sell its land, bring in the new populace, create farms and cities, and

thereby provide a profitable, self-perpetuating business for itself.
Bypassing the Union Pacific, which already traversed central Nebraska, the Burlington concentrated on the lands south of the Platte,
where competition was virtually nonexistent; and the company del-
uged the East with pamphlets, handbills, posters, brochures, and
circulars propagandizing the western movement.

Millions of acres were advertised for sale on ten years' credit at 6
percent with no payment on principal during the first four years.
Throughout the East, Canada, and Europe were distributed one
hundred thousand territorial maps describing Nebraska as "a garden
patch" and "a sea of wheat"—the best farming and stock-raising
country in the world because of its ideal soil, water, and climate. So
successful was the Burlington that by the end of 1872 not only had it
sold more than three hundred thousand acres at $7.50 net an acre,
but it had hauled in that year a quarter of a million bushels of wheat
from Nebraska to Chicago.[1]

As the railroad spread iron fingers pell mell toward the Colorado
mountains, it hurriedly established "towns" as it went along to be
watering spots for engines and camps for rail gangs. And the places
were named, hastily, in alphabetical order—from Crete to Fairmont
to Hastings to Juniata—so that in a sense the towns were there
before the people. Otherwise, west of Lincoln lay raw prairie, mile
after mile of vast, tawny land on which man had scarcely left his
mark. A plain of alluvial soil rolled five hundred miles from east to
west, potentially the breadbasket of a continent, watered by slug-
gish, muddy rivers. Merging with a small independent line in the
Republican Valley, the Burlington reached the tiny settlement of
Red Cloud. From this outpost the merging lines were joined by a
north-south spur to Hastings, thereby opening an area of two
hundred and fifty thousand acres for settlement. In brochures and
placards the Burlington advised, "Go and See for Yourself. You will
be Convinced, as Thousands have been Before You." These new
lands lay in the midst of what its agents described colorfully as the
"Gulf Stream of Migration," an immense and largely imaginary
Utopia whose border on the north was the Aurora Borealis and on
the south the Day of Judgment.[2]

II   A Child's Virginia

As a family, the Cathers were established in America during Co-
lonial days when Jasper Cather came from Ireland. His great grand-

son was Charles Cather, who lived at the family home, Willow Shade Farm, near Back Creek Valley in the hill country west of Winchester. On her maternal side Willa Cather's forebears were also Virginian; her grandmother, Rachel Seibert of Back Creek Valley, had married William Boak, a United States government official, had lived with him in Washington, and had borne him five children. At Boak's death Rachel, then thirty-eight, returned home with her children, among whom was Mary Virginia Boak, who married Charles Cather on December 5, 1872. The newlyweds lived with Mrs. Boak, and their first daughter was born at her home a year later, on December 7, 1873. Christened Wilella, but usually called "Willie" among her family, she invented the name Willa for herself as she matured; and since her parents had omitted a middle name, she eventually adopted that of the maternal line, spelling it "Sibert."

The first Cathers to take up the Burlington's offer were George Cather and his wife, Frances—Willa Cather's uncle and aunt—who left for the West in 1873, shortly prior to their niece's birth. By the time Willa Cather was a year old, they had established their homestead in south-central Nebraska. Their tract was located on the plateau between the Little Blue and the Republican rivers northwest of the new Red Cloud community that was situated on the high ground that is familiar to readers of Cather stories as "the Divide." Because the territory—however attractively planned and plotted on the railroad's maps—lacked settlements, roads, or other reliable landmarks, the Cathers followed others' example in finding their way: they tied a rag to the rim of their wagon wheel and headed their team in the correct compass direction from the tiny railroad depot at Juniata, which lay just past Hastings. Knowing the circumference of the wheel, they had only to keep count of its revolutions to ascertain the distance traveled. On a treeless plain characterized by an undemarcated rug of shaggy reddish grass, there was no other way.

Despite the hardships of life on the Divide, the Cathers had come to stay, and their region soon was known by the unofficial title of "Catherton." Willa's grandparents soon joined the Nebraska entourage, allowing Charles and his family to move into the big house on Willow Shade Farm. Soon Mrs. Boak joined them, and for eight years they lived in the brick home, farming and raising sheep. By 1883 the family included Willa's brothers Roscoe and Douglass as well as her sister Jessica. In that year the enormous sheep barn at Willow Shade burned to the ground. Discouraged, Willa's father could no longer resist the tug of the West. An auction disposed of the family property and farm equipment and raised $6,000 for the adventure.[3]

III   *On the Divide*

Of all seasons March was the most depressing time of the year to encounter Nebraska. With its white mask of snow melted away and with spring's greenery not yet apparent, the flat land was at its bleakest: frozen solid as the bricks on the depot platform if the cold lingered or sloggy with mud if the thaw had begun. Willa Cather, nine years old, was left with indelible impressions: sheet iron, that was what this land looked like, or naked, like the back of her hand. The encounter mingled excitement with terror within her, as if she had wandered to the precipitous edge of the world. When the family set out in an open Studebaker wagon pointed toward Catherton—a slow, jolting trip—the uninhabited territory gripped her. "I was sitting on the hay," she remembered, "holding on to the side of the wagon box to steady myself—the roads were mostly faint trails over the bunch grass in those days. The land was open range and there was almost no fencing. As we drove further and further out into the country, I felt a good deal as if we had come to the end of everything—it was a kind of erasure of personality."[4] Her major resolve was to maintain her courage and, under any circumstances, not to cry; with the help of an occasional meadowlark, whose song gave life to the dead landscape, she succeeded.

Charles Cather had told his daughter that one needed "grit," and on this trip to Catherton she began to understand what he meant. But after the family had settled on the Divide and during the eighteen months they spent there, she was thoroughly impressed with the precise degree of grit required of the settlers pouring in to make Webster County an outpost of the civilized world. Grandmother Boak, as an example, found it essential to do her gardening armed with a hickory cane, steel tipped for killing the rattlesnakes that still nested in the area. To utilize the rich cropland beneath, a thick covering of native sod had to be removed, a back-breaking job. The sod peeled off like peat, with roots knotted together from decades of growth making it cohesive enough to be used for many of the first homes. Cut into blocks, it provided thick walls both to insulate against summer heat and to withstand winter gales. Some settlers, of course, lived in dugouts not much different from caves, for only the genuinely affluent could afford to haul in the lumber necessary for a wooden house. Fortunately, the Cather grandparents chose to return to Virginia for an extended visit, and Charles and his family were able to occupy their wooden house.

Among the Cathers' many surprises was the discovery that native-born Americans were in the minority on the Divide. The Burlington's net had indeed been flung wide: as early as 1869 the railroad had planned for overseas distribution of Nebraska land pamphlets in English, German, Danish, and Scandinavian. Another distribution in 1873 added French and Bohemian language versions. During the 1870s Nebraska grew by 310 percent, and it was no accident that foreign settlement comprised the majority of this growth. In fact, twenty-three nations were represented among the purchasers of Burlington land, led by immigrants from Bohemia, Denmark, Germany, Russia, and Sweden. These people left a deep impression on Willa Cather, who found their colonies "spread across our bronze prairies like the daubs of color on a painter's palette," and they provided opportunities for contact on every hand: "On Sunday we could drive to a Norwegian church and listen to a sermon in that language, or to a Danish or a Swedish church. We could go to the French Catholic settlement in the next county and hear a sermon in French, or into the Bohemian township and hear one in Czech, or we could go to church with the German Lutherans."[5] There were native American colonies also, but these lacked exotic color and did not rouse her curiosity.

The Europeans, with their national garb, odd tongues, and intriguing manners, were another matter. "I liked them from the first," said Willa Cather, "and they made up for what I missed in the country." Wives, mothers, and daughters who had sacrificed homes overseas in order to pioneer a new continent were in a position to understand the Virginia child's hunger for the security left behind her in Shenandoah country. She gravitated to them for her comfort, and they provided it. She took from them also her first inklings of the Old World. On the pony her father put at her disposal, she followed buffalo trails across the prairie to visit them and to hear their stories. Even if the conversations came to her in unfamiliar tongues, she forced herself to comprehend. "I have never," she said, "found any intellectual excitement any more intense than I

used to feel when I spent a morning with one of those old women at
her baking or butter making. I used to ride home in the most
unreasonable state of excitement." And this statement was made
after she had been through the university, served as managing
editor of a national magazine, visited the major cities of America,
and traveled to Europe at least three times.[6]

With a child's natural instinct for exploration, Willa Cather accli-
mated herself rapidly. If she tired of the dugouts and the soddies
where her foreigners lived, she had the buffalo wallows to investigate. The big herds were gone, but there remained depressions
worn by their hooves and packed by their rolling until they held
water as if they had cement bottoms. Meandering creeks where
native cottonwoods grew were magnets also; any tree in this largely
treeless land became a curiosity. And there were ravines that
sunflowers filled with midsummer color and the remnants of old
lagoons golden with coreopsis. By the end of her first autumn at
Catherton, the shaggy-grass country already looked much different,
for she was looking at it with another pair of eyes. It was her home,
and, despite its terrifying aspects, she had come to love it. The land
had gripped her attention, her emotions, with a passion she never
escaped.

The chapter of Willa Cather's life in which she was free to come
and go at will and to taste life fully on her own was ending. In the
wide net cast by the railroad, many were caught who proved poorly
suited to frontier conditions; not everyone could adjust to the rough
life of the Divide. Some pushed further West, searching for the El
Dorado that lay at the end of every Westerner's trail; others
packed—or sold out—and crawled back to the East; and the less
resourceful often suffered tragedy. Willa Cather heard of the sad
fate that befell a Bohemian farmer—a would-be farmer, actually, for
he had been a violinist in Prague and could not manage the change
to drastic new conditions. In despair he had smashed his fiddle, his
single solace against the unanticipated wildness of the country; had
then shot himself; and had been buried at a crossroads. The story of
this suicide, Francis Sadilek, haunted her.

Among those inadequately suited for homesteading was Willa
Cather's own father, who found his new life much more precarious
than he had anticipated. Catherton was hardly a "place" at all. The
nearest medical care was fourteen difficult miles away, and for the
Cather children the three-month school term was inadequate. On

September 11, 1884, the Red Cloud newspaper announced: "Public sale of Charles Cather will be held 14 miles northwest of Red Cloud and 9 miles north of Inavale, Section 22, Township 3, Range 12, on Monday, September 22."[7] Everything—cattle, horses, hogs, wagons, plows, machinery—was put on the block. The sale accomplished, Charles Cather prepared to go into business in Red Cloud.

IV *Red Cloud*

When Willa Cather first lived there in 1884, Red Cloud was a prairie town of some twenty-five hundred inhabitants. That the immigrant strain was present in Red Cloud, as well as on the Divide, is not surprising, considering that as late as 1910 more than nine hundred thousand of Nebraska's million plus inhabitants were foreign born. Only fourteen years old, the town was known already for its churches and schools. Webster Street's false-front wooden structures, typical of frontier main streets, were being augmented by more permanent brick buildings. Plans were well underway for an Opera House in which organizations might gather or road companies perform. With Red Cloud evolving into an important stop on the Burlington route to Denver, an Opera House was indispensable to entice traveling notables to linger long enough to address the citizenry.

The Cathers found a house on Third and Cedar Streets, just off Webster. Not too well planned or built, the house was long and narrow, a story and a half in height; it had been constructed by a lumberman who, Willa Cather was always convinced, cared more for profit than for planning. She surmised he had built on speculation and had used secondhand and leftover pieces from his lumberyard. But the house was available and convenient, and the family moved in: parents; children; Grandmother Boak; Bess Seymour, who was Mrs. Cather's cousin; and the hired girl, Marjorie Anderson.[8] Two downstairs bedrooms in the cramped house were used by the parents and by Grandmother Boak, and an unfinished "dormitory" upstairs accommodated the children. When Willa was a teenager, part of this upper floor was partitioned to form a private cubicle for her.

The most important fact was that the new house was in a town with civilized comforts, accessible education and medical care, and easy contact with people. Willa Cather became friends with the girls down the block, the Miners, whose father ran a grand new brick establishment on Webster Street known as The Store. The four girls—Carrie, Irene, Margie, and Mary—offered Willa the friendship any new girl in town needs; and she, always a leader, was soon casting them in plays composed by herself and performed in the Cather dormitory attic and in the Miner parlor. When Willa Cather was fourteen in 1888, her troupe presented "Beauty and the Beast" downtown in the Opera House as a benefit for victims of that winter's historic blizzard.[9]

Whether staging one of her own playlets, reciting "Hiawatha" dressed in Indian garb, or trekking the mile to the depot to welcome one of the half dozen stock companies that each winter played in Red Cloud, Willa Cather's instinct was to reach beyond the confines of the town, beyond the prairie, beyond Nebraska—to what no one could yet suggest. Long after these girlhood days had passed, Carrie Miner Sherwood, with whom Willa had remained fast friends, insisted that the girls knew their neighbor would go places—not that they anticipated her writing career, specifically, "but we knew she would be *something* unusual, something *special*."[10] The immigrants Willa Cather encountered in town were better educated, more "citified," and certainly more affluent than the sodbusters, but they were no less intriguing or valuable. The Miner girls' mother, as an example, had been born in Christiana (later Oslo), Norway, daughter of an oboeist in the Royal Norwegian Orchestra conducted by Ole Bull. She was short, blonde, stout, and—true to her childhood environment—a music lover. One of Willa Cather's fond memories was of Mrs. Miner's fat little fingers skipping over the keyboard of her piano. At one time she hired an itinerant musician to teach piano to her daughters, and Mrs. Cather employed him as well. Although Willa possessed little native talent and cherished no ambition for a musical career, music remained a passionate lifelong interest.

Another local merchant, Charles Wiener, whose wife was French, possessed the most extraordinary private library in Red Cloud: French classics, the German edition of Scott's novels, and English translations of Schiller. The Wieners, who conversed easily in French and German, inspired their young neighbor to learn French herself, not so much in order to speak with them perhaps as o read the books, for Willa had been allowed the run of the library.

"One of the people who interested me the most," Willa Cather later said, was Annie Sadilek, the Bohemian hired girl from the farming territory who worked at the Miners. Annie carried the spirit of the Divide into town, and she became for Willa the archetype of an open and life-loving human being whose spirit remained impervious both to the harsh life on the prairie, where her father had recently died, and to her utter lack of means. Literally without possession, she apparently hungered for nothing, and this fact, in a society already exhibiting a predilection for things, set her apart. Her life taught Willa Cather that an individual can rise above circumstance, that one can to an extent create his own conditions, and that happiness is decided by one's capacity for enjoyment.

At the Miners Annie Sadilek learned to cook and to sew, and eventually most of the clothes worn by her brothers and sisters back on the homestead came from her hands. Her family collected the small wages she earned, and if the Miners had not retained enough to purchase her a pair of shoes, she would have continued wearing the oilcloth and denim slippers she stitched for herself. To Willa, this free spirit was intriguing, and she loitered at the Miner home observing Annie's cheerful ways, admiring her energy, and marveling at the phenomenon of an ignorant, penniless girl becoming a magnet for the young men of Red Cloud. Reaching womanhood, Annie married a farmer and raised a large family on whom she lavished the same fullness of spirit. Over the years Willa Cather clung to this Bohemian girl as closely as to any of her childhood friends.[11]

Among Willa's other friends and acquaintances who left permanent impressions was Miss Evangeline King, principal of the South Ward School during the Cathers' second year in Red Cloud. "I wanted more than any thing else in the world to please her," said Willa, who relied on her guidance even after she was attending the high school. Later, Miss King became Superintendent of Public Instruction for all of Webster County, and she eventually joined the faculty of Kearney State Teachers' College.

Illustrious citizens of Red Cloud were the Garbers, in whose imposing home Willa Cather was often a guest. Silas Garber had been among the founders of the town—it was his suggestion to name it after the Sioux chief—and in 1873 he had been elected governor of the state. A widower, he had met a young beauty in California whom he had married and brought to the governor's mansion, where her youth and vivacity established her reputation as the most

remarkable official hostess Lincoln had known. The gubernatorial
term over, the Garbers returned to Red Cloud and their home in
the cottonwood grove on a knoll just beyond town. Here Lyra
Garber cared for her husband, a good deal older than she, who had
been injured in a carriage accident. Whenever health permitted,
they entertained, and Willa Cather appears to have been welcome
at their home whenever they were not traveling. She remembered
Lyra Garber as "a flash of brightness in a grey background," and the
story of her romance with the governor, so distant from anything
Willa herself was ever to experience, enchanted—and mystified—
her.[12]

Willa Cather grew to young womanhood enjoying her friends,
observing human nature closely, learning from everyone within her
range, and reading widely in her home library and at the Wieners.
She was capable at fourteen of identifying her hobbies as "Snakes &
Sheakspear,"[13] in itself an indication of the growing-up process she
was passing through, a spectrum that included a crew-cut, tomboy
period (her family and friends had long called her "Willie") and her
early ambition to become a medical doctor. While engrossed with
medicine, Willa thought surgery a likely specialty, and she began to
practice by dissecting frogs and toads, which were abundant and
easily caught. Such bloody activities raised a hue and cry of cruelty
among the genteel of Red Cloud, but Willa Cather did not relent.
When the time came for her to graduate (one of three in the high
school class of 1890), she stood in the local opera house and formally
compounded her offense by reciting an original oration in defense of
open and free experimentation. Under her title, "Superstition versus Investigation," Willa asked the people of Red Cloud to consider
where the nation's future experts might be expected to come from if
novices were barred from instruction. For her, the life destroyed in
experimentation since the beginning of time was as nothing compared with the benefits accruing from a single great discovery, the
circulation of the blood. The young who examined, and even dissec-
ted, the things of nature that surrounded them were not triflers, she
insisted, nor were they cruel. On the contrary, "It is the most sacred
right of man to investigate"; it is, further, "the hope of our age."[14]

A most remarkable salvo to be fired by one so young. And in its
way it marked Willa Cather's farewell not only to high school but to
the town. She was eager to extend her horizons beyond Red Cloud,
and her first step toward doing so involved a hundred-mile rail

journey east to Lincoln, where she hoped to be accepted by the state university. She was just sixteen years old.

V *Maverick on the Campus*

The University of Nebraska in 1890 was a typical prairie college in appearance—a motley collection of red brick buildings spaced on open, flat land. In the fashion of the times, pretentious gothic and romanesque towers adorned the four college structures, making them look disproportionately tall, particularly against the recent plantings that they dwarfed on the treeless plain. But Lincoln itself was an instant city; in comparison with any other community in the region, its population of thirty thousand made it a metropolis. It lay on the main route of the Burlington, a necessity in an era when few towns could hope to survive if not easily accessible by rail. To accommodate travelers and to serve those arriving in town on government business, there were five hotels; to entertain them, two theaters, each boasting a capacity in excess of one thousand.

Because the rudimentary Red Cloud schools did not yet furnish an adequate precollege education, Willa Cather was unable to matriculate at once as a regular university student. Instead, she was assigned to a "prep" class for young people from outland schools. Sailing through her preparatory year, she became in the fall of 1891 a full-fledged freshman. Hers was not a large beginning class; but judged by modern standards, the university itself was miniscule, enrolling less than four hundred students altogether. Yet for Willa Cather the campus was magic, a true wonderland, led by professors whose wide learning and varied abilities promised to open exciting new windows on the world.

A young English instructor, Herbert Bates, just out of Harvard University, brought to the campus the attractive aura of the East. He helped Willa Cather publish her first serious writing ventures. Louise Pound, already known as an Anglo-Saxon scholar, and her brother Roscoe, who would go on to become the dean of Harvard Law School, were on the faculty. So was John J. Pershing; then an ROTC lieutenant, he was destined to lead the American Expeditionary Forces in World War I. The university itself was led by Chancellor James Canfield, who was attracted from Kansas and who later headed Ohio State University. Joining the student body was his daughter, who as Dorothy Canfield Fisher would become a writer and be awarded the Pulitzer Prize. Dorothy Canfield and

Willa collaborated on a football story, "The Fear that Walks by Noonday," for the college yearbook, *The Sombrero*, of which Willa was editor in 1894. Dorothy supplied the plot; her friend did the writing.

Nearly fifty years after graduation, Willa Cather's classmates were asked by James Shively to push aside the cobwebs of half a century and share their impressions of her. Like Willa herself, many by that time were dead, but twenty-one of the survivors did respond; and almost without exception those who had known her at all recognized that an individualist had worked in their midst. Willa Cather's appearance, of course, set her apart, for she had adopted a mannish look that was daring for the times. One former student recalled sharing a double desk in English class with Willa, who wore a tailored suit coat from whose sleeves peeped the white cuffs of a starched shirt and whose high stiff collar was adorned by a four-in-hand necktie—this in the era of the Gibson Girl. Her shingled hair and severe apparel dominated the memories of fully two-thirds of those who were on campus with her. Although her "uniform" suggests a symbolic protest against male favoritism, in conversation she "affected the slang expressions used by the boys. She said that her name, Willa, was the feminine of William."[15]

Willa Cather's former classmates were prone to recall her as unhandsome, somewhat thickset; but her face was usually remembered as "unusually alert and intelligent." Jasper Hunt, precise in his memory, was rather more favorably disposed than the majority: "Her face was not one of doll-like beauty, but was strong and good to look at, brunette but rather light. Her voice was somewhat low-pitched, at least alto, and her hearty laugh was rich and reminded you of nutty flavors."[16] Few came to know her well, for she restricted her circle from innate shyness or a sense of personal exclusiveness. Her motives were not clear even to those who knew her well. Many knew her only by reputation or to greet with the traditional "Good morning" while crossing campus, and the casually connected were apt to feel insulted. "I well remember . . . her superior air" was a typical comment, and after fifty years one classmate continued to resent Willa's outspoken criticism of "everyone on the campus" in her *Daily Nebraskan* column; this fellow student concluded that Willa "had no friends and wanted none."[17]

This statement was a gross misjudgment, for no one ever

hungered more for good companionship than Willa Cather. "One clings to one's friends so," she told a reporter in later years. At the same time, she cultivated most those who might help her in some fashion to grow intellectually or artistically. She was too much in a hurry to do otherwise. Great demands were made on her friends; nothing less than complete fidelity would do. "Willa was reserved and indifferent to ordinary people and consequently appeared to be rather lonely," suggested B. C. Mathews, who knew her better than some, having served with her on the *Hesperian* staff; but "she was not," he added, "a snob."[18]

The portrait of Willa Cather as a college student builds in ambiguities. She was much in evidence but little known; aggressive but intelligent; friendly or standoffish; arrogant or kind; liked but not loved; plain or pleasant to see. One classmate suggested that the tendency of youth to be hypercritical ("We were quite mid-Victorian") caused Willa's oddness to be noted more than her intellect. But concerning innate ability, there is no disagreement, even among the few who actively disliked her; "brilliant," "energetic," "mature," "assertive," "independent," "self-confident, positive, alert, vivacious" are recurrent adjectives. An awareness of the Cather ambition figures prominently in these thumbnail memoirs—and the ambitious are seldom lovable. Few were taken unaware by her later achievement, for she seemed even then to know her objectives and to be pursuing them diligently. A student who deeply resented her apparent uncordiality on the Lincoln campus offered a remark that says perhaps all that needs to be said of the author during her collegiate days. It came in a pair of balanced phrases: *"She was very egotistical: really had the right to be!"*[19]

VI *A Fledgling Artist*

While at the university, Willa Cather made her first tentative moves toward a writing career. Two campus literary magazines, the *Lasso,* on which she served with Louise Pound as associate editor, and the *Hesperian,* for which she was associate editor and later managing editor, were her training ground. She broke into print early and unexpectedly when an essay written in her freshman year so impressed her instructor, Ebenezer Hunt, that he arranged to have it printed in a leading Lincoln newspaper, the *Nebraska State Journal.* Later it was reprinted in the *Hesperian.* Within a few months the *Journal* took a second Cather essay, "Shakespeare and Hamlet."

Simultaneously she experimented with fiction. In later life her tendency was to disown these attempts altogether, to pretend they didn't exist, and to take every precaution against their being unearthed or reprinted. But she was candid in 1921 in telling a journalist that "back in the files of the college magazine, there were once several of my perfectly honest but very clumsy attempts to give the story of some of the Scandinavian and Bohemian settlers who lived not far from my father's farm. In these sketches, I simply tried to tell about the people, without much regard for style."[20]

Amateurish though these stories are, they are important in identifying Cather's natural materials, which later reappear, refined, in her major stories and novels. Her first tale, "Peter," is little more than a sketched reminiscence of the Francis Sadilek suicide, colored by youthful imagination. Naming her hero Peter Sadelack, she pictures him as a Prague violinist wrecked by a paralytic stroke shortly after being transported from his native Bohemia to a southwestern Nebraska claim. His son Antone manages the homestead while Peter, drinking heavily to obliterate his sorrows in this wasteland of "nothin but sun, and grass, and sky," daydreams of his lost life. His son and wife threaten to sell his violin, unused since his stroke. One cold winter's night when their threats become intolerable, Peter smashes the instrument rather than see it sold, and squatting on the dirt floor of his sod hut with "the wolves howling in the distance, and the night wind screaming," he places his son's shotgun between his knees, rests the muzzle against his temple, and employs his toe to pull the trigger. Even before the funeral the son treks to town to sell the violin bow that Peter had neglected to break. "Bald" and "emotional," the adjectives Cather used in dismissing the story, suit it well. But the story paints an extremely harsh picture not at all unlike the literary naturalism popularized in the 1890s by Hamlin Garland in his grim stories of Iowa and Dakota farm life.

With the help of Herbert Bates, "Peter" was sent to Boston to a little magazine called the *Mahogany Tree*. Wonder of wonders, it was accepted; at eighteen Willa Cather was a published author of fiction! Impressed, the editors of the *Hesperian* asked permission to reprint "Peter" and did so; but it did not appear until the November issue—a month after publication of a second story Willa had given them. "Lou, the Prophet" told of another Nebraska immigrant, this one a Dane, who settled in a dugout on his land claim, who worked from daybreak to sunset to scratch out a living, and whose head was awhirl with memories. In this story—one as unrelenting as Peter's— Lou's life is said to be "as sane and as uneventful as the life of his plowhorses, and . . . as hard and thankless." Eventually it becomes unbearable. When drouth withers his crops, he faces ruination. Deranged, he thinks that the wickedness of man has called God's wrath upon the earth, and to him the shriveling of his corn forecasts a world fiery with cleansing flame. Madness sets in. Hunted by the local constabulary, Lou disappears, drowned perhaps in the shallow remains of the river, his body trapped by quicksand. Again, the grimness of the details reflects Willa Cather's first strong, fearful impressions of the untamed Divide in themes of failure, despair, madness.

Other experiments followed, and the three published by the *Hesperian* during 1892 and 1893 are less typical and even less successful. "A Tale of the White Pyramid"—not unlike the historical and speculative fiction popular in the era of *Ben-Hur* and *She*—tells of the burial of Pharoah Senefrau and the sealing of his tomb. In this tale the romantic strain in Cather appears, and she poured into it her reading in the manners and customs of ancient Egypt. "A Son of the Celestial," which concerns the life of a Chinaman in San Francisco, also stems from her reading and not her experience. A third tale, "The Clemency of the Court," returns to Nebraska immigrant materials. Serge Povilitchky is the illegitimate son of a Russian girl in a western railroad colony who drowns herself when Serge is but months old. This beginning sets the tone for Serge's story: a persecuted boyhood, full-time work at age twelve, friendship only of a stray dog. When the dog is killed by Serge's sadistic employer, Serge hatchets him in retaliation. He is jailed; after torture he is strangled in prison. The Cather notion of prison life is surely imaginary, but her portrait of Serge belongs with those of Peter and Lou: all are foreigners destroyed by the frontier.[21]

VII *Girl with a Meat Ax*

Campus publications provided Willa Cather with a meager enough stage on which to perform but one that was sufficient to her needs until her junior year, when she received a proposal from the *Nebraska State Journal* about contributing a regular column. She enthusiastically accepted this offer, and, as a result, she composed local color sketches that reflected her curiosity about the life around

her. Soon she was given the more challenging assignment of reviewing theatrical productions in the Lincoln theaters. At the time she
began, in December 1893, a rival paper had condemned local criticism as "a dreary waste of undiluted mediocrity" tossed off by men
devoid of any standards for significant judgments. Willa Cather
changed all that: before long, troupes playing Lincoln became aware
that nothing short of their very best would do; anything less would
provoke the smoking pen of the *Journal*'s new, young critic to roast
them in print. Two years of Willa Cather's weekly column, which
she called "The Passing Show," earned her a reputation sufficiently
widespread for the Des Moines *Register* to comment that Lincoln
could claim the best theatrical criticism in the West.[22]

Immaturity sometimes causes a beginning critic, particularly a
young one, to swing toward extremes: he can lavish enthusiasm
indiscriminately, or he can maintain standards which no one will
ever quite achieve. Willa Cather tended toward the latter. Although
she had attended a good number of productions while in Lincoln,
Nebraska lay an immense distance from the heart of American stage
activity, and the Broadway standards against which boondocks companies might be measured were hers only in imagination. Nonethe-
less, she never hesitated to judge rigorously. When she wrote of one
troupe, "All *Uncle Tom's Cabin* companies are bad, this being one of
the worst," she risked little, of course; "Tom Shows" by the 1890s
were notorious for their melodramatics and ineptness. But when
more unique companies visited, she was capable of the same ex-
tremities; in fact, she could be furious when she thought a third-rate
production was being palmed off on the outlands. When Rider Hag-
gard's pseudo-science fantasy *She* came to town, she castigated both
play and players. Its hero, Edwin Brown, struck her as "corpulent
and stagy," and she said so; "he could not even read his lines intelligently." The heroine herself was "quite pretty—when she had her
veil on"; but she, like her co-star, "was utterly incapable of reading
her lines." The play itself was damned as being "as awful as the
people who play it."[23]

No limits bound Willa Cather's impatience with stock companies
who dared bring to Lincoln the outworn wares unacceptable elsewhere, and she assumed no responsibility for padding an actor's
scrapbook with happy notices. The heroine of *Cleopatra*, Lillian
Lewis, would be unlikely to clip a review that described her as
walking like a milkmaid and as moving like a housemaid. Apparently

finding this damnation insufficient, Willa continued a week later: "I
have seen waiters in restaurants who were ten times more queenly.
Her movements were exactly like those of the women who give you
Turkish baths in Chicago." The twenty-one-year-old critic had recently spent a week in Chicago, but the extent of her experience in
Turkish baths remains undocumented. According to the *Journal*'s
managing editor, Will Owen Jones, the awful Miss Cather threw a
scare into actors from coast to coast. Players in Lincoln slept badly,
never knowing what new assault to expect from "that meatax young
girl."[24]

Of course, she would not have lasted for long without some appropriate tempering, and when a performance called for it, she
could praise as lavishly as she could condemn. When *Hamlet* came
to town, she found Walker Whiteside's prince "strong, manly, self-
contained"; and Louis James' acting in *Falstaff* was "entirely satisfying . . . coarse without being vulgar." Richard Mansfield, for Willa
Cather a rare master, evoked her highest admiration with a vocal
range matched by an ability, as she put it, to make even his silences
speak. He played Beau Brummell with faultless skill—so much the
consummate gentleman "one knows that he even sleeps with elegance."[25]

The possibility of flawless artistry was beginning to engross Cather's mind, and she commented of Mansfield's performances that one
was left with little to say when faced by real art. Of a perfect work,
only another artist might describe the how or why. Such "asides"
began early in Cather's reviews, and in them can be seen the young
artist testing her own wings; reaching for an ideal, determined to
soar; and setting for herself the highest standards.

A year of arduous play reviewing convinced Willa Cather that the
actor's was the hardest of all lives led for art, his product needing to
be created anew for each performance, something comparable to a
painter's being required to finish a new canvas every evening. The
evanescence of the performing arts both inspired and appalled her.
Each perfect creation bloomed for its brief hour and then vanished
"as music dies in a broken lute"; when the actor dies, his greatness
perishes.[26] More reassuring was the career of a writer. He might
labor and die, but he had the hope of posthumous influence. As her
graduation day approached, Willa Cather chose not an actor but a
writer to be the topic for her address before the university literary
societies.

Significantly she chose a prose master, the author of "the first perfect short stories in the English language," Edgar Allan Poe. In retrospect, her decision has the air of inevitability, she herself being drawn to a life dedicated to the literary art. In Poe she saw the life of art at its most demanding, yet its most unadulterated. Friendless, often hungry, plagued by creditors, crippled by alcoholism, and doomed to observe the wreckage of those he most loved, Poe never allowed the flag of his art to be sullied. That he was a liar and an egoist mattered little to Willa Cather, for the man was nothing; his work, everything: "There is so little perfection." By 1895 all that mattered was that somehow, against all odds, Poe had kept the ideal of perfect work. "I have wondered so often how he did it," Cather said in her speech. "How he kept his purpose always clean and his taste always perfect."

Whether she realized it or not, Willa Cather already had her answer embedded in her eulogy to Poe—his single-mindedness evidenced in his refusal to become discouraged, deflected, or side-tracked. But in 1895, still at the first step of her own journey, she could not yet state this answer as a certainty. She needed to live the life of art herself in order to confirm what she had said about Poe.[27]

VIII *The Best Years*

In 1921 Willa Cather described a book as being "cremated youth"; and she told a journalist that the years from eight to fifteen are the formative period of a writer's life, for then he unconsciously gathers basic material.[28] If this be true, then her first experiences in the West might be expected to figure prominently in her fiction. And they do, beginning with the Sadilek suicide that she first heard about in her ninth year, experimented with in "Peter," and later made an important episode in *My Ántonia*. This novel, along with *O Pioneers!* and *The Song of the Lark*, centers on the immigrants whom Willa Cather knew on the Divide and in Red Cloud. The Divide itself, of course, is the locale for all the farm scenes in novels from *O Pioneers!* through *One of Ours*, as well as for those in short stories such as "Neighbour Rosicky." And the town serves pseud-onymously for all the small Western towns of the novels: Hanover in *O Pioneers!*, Moonstone in *The Song of the Lark*, Black Hawk in *My Ántonia*, Frankfort in *One of Ours*, Sweet Water in *A Lost Lady*, and Haverford in *Lucy Gayheart*.

Carrie Miner Sherwood was told that an author created characters from living models to which a portion of the writer's self had been added; and Willa Cather reminded her that Lucy Gayheart was based upon a girl, known to both of them, who skated on Nebraska's winter ponds dressed in red jersey. The story "Two Friends" did not present a portrait of Mr. Miner of Red Cloud but of Mr. Miner as he seemed to twelve-year-old Willa Cather, which is another matter. And Ántonia Shimerda, though drawn primarily from the Miners' hired girl, Anna Sadilek, represented all that Cather felt about those who pioneered the prairie.[29] The character most nearly a portrait is that of Mrs. Harling in *My Antonia,* a character based upon Cather's reminiscences of Mrs. Miner.[30] Carrie Miner Sherwood herself was the prototype for Thea Kronborg's friend, Frances Harling, and her sisters for the other Harling girls.

Other parallels occur frequently. Aunt Georgiana, who heard the music program in "A Wagner Matinée," was based upon her aunt Frances Cather, the first of the family to settle on the Divide. The Charles Weiners, who let Willa use their library, enter the story "Old Mrs. Harris" as Mr. and Mrs. Rosen. Silas Garber, the ex-governor, and his wife Lyra suggest Captain and Mrs. Forrester of *A Lost Lady.* Margie Anderson, the hired girl who accompanied the Cathers from Virginia, is cast in *One of Ours* as old Mahailey, in *The Professor's House* as Augusta, and in "Old Mrs. Harris" as Mandy. Evangeline King, Willa's favorite teacher, emerges in "The Best Years" as Evangeline Knightly.[31]

Willa Cather herself appears in countless elements of her own stories; for example, much of her ambition and drive goes into the making of Thea Kronborg, and the experiences of Claude Wheeler in Lincoln are essentially Cather's own experiences. Hers also are the attitudes expressed toward the people and the land. The opening description in *O Pioneers!* of Hanover, "anchored on a windy Nebraska tableland . . . trying not to be blown away," captures the sense of fear Willa Cather had felt as a child that her family had brought her to a precarious land beyond the edge of the world itself.

CHAPTER 2

From Nebraska to the World

> "You must know the world before you
> can know the village."
> —Miss Jewett to Willa Cather, 1908

I *Pittsburgh*

UPON graduation from the University of Nebraska in 1895, Willa Cather had earned a journalistic reputation in Lincoln and even beyond. Taking note of this fact, the weekly Lincoln *Courier* invited her in August to join its staff part-time; and she was soon writing both for it and for the *Journal*. Her hopes were high. The *Nebraska Editor* cited her as one certain to become known on a wide scale, and the *Weekly Express* in Beatrice identified her as a writer soon to have a national reputation.[1] During this time Willa chose to live in Red Cloud and mail her work to the newspapers, going to Lincoln only on visits or to cover the theatrical season. However, it became apparent to her that she would not make her mark nationally in this manner. She lacked really engrossing, full-time employment in Lincoln, and life in her smaller hometown seemed comparable to Siberian exile. A trickle of publications included her depressing story of the Catherton region, "On the Divide," in the *Overland Monthly,* her first recognition by a magazine of national circulation.

But her forward movement had to wait until late spring 1896, when the *Home Monthly,* a small Pittsburgh magazine, offered her a post. On June 17 the *Journal* carried the news that its dramatic critic would go East "for a couple of months," thereby implying that she would be back in Lincoln at summer's end. Whether Cather intended to return is highly doubtful, for she hoped to remain in the East; her postcollege year had strained the limits of her Nebraska opportunities. Unfortunately, as she had recognized in her oration on Poe, one's living had to be made: "Bread seems a little thing to stand in the way of genius, but it can."[2]

The writing Willa Cather did for *Home Monthly* was of the fleeting variety, but there was enough of it to keep her busy. The magazine was brand new, having been established in 1894 as *Ladies' Journal* and then renamed in 1896, when Charles Axtell purchased it. Axtell employed Cather as an assistant editor, which meant, as she soon discovered, that he expected her to serve as jack-of-all-trades. This intent became clear soon after her arrival in Pittsburgh when Axtell took a vacation and left her to supervise the publication of the magazine's first issue under its new name. Since insufficient copy existed in the files, she was obliged to write much of what appeared in the August issue; and she also had to help the inexperienced printers at the press itself. She did not mind. If she was writing trivia, she was writing full-time; and a compensation occurred to her—the use of *Home Monthly* to print stories she was writing on her own. After the indecision of the past year, she was as busy as she ever hoped to be; not a moment did she have for boredom or regret.

Since no obstacle blocked her use of *Home Monthly* as a ready vehicle for her stories, Cather began at once to insert them among its mundane columns. The August 1896 issue carried two, one of which, "Tommy, the Unsentimental," is indicative of her new feeling toward Nebraska: her fear of its hostile environment is mitigated by her maturing appreciation of its wild attractiveness. The contrived love-story plot of "Tommy" is set in Nebraska, and the action occurs on a summer day when the sun of "hot brass" and a searing wind from the south have produced the "sickening, destroying heat" she knew so well from Catherton Augusts. Yet Theodosia (whose nickname "Tommy" suggests Willa's nickname "Willie"), recently returned from school in the East, finds herself "mighty homesick" for the huge blue sky, the vast plains, and even for "this hateful, dear old, everlasting wind that comes down like the sweep of cavalry and is never tamed or broken."[3] There was something good, at last, about the frontier; but Cather had to leave the scene to realize it.

In Pittsburgh Willa Cather was impressed less by the steel kings' stranglehold on civic affairs than by the cultural life that their rapacity had made possible. The singers, the dramas, and the Carnegie Hall recitals and concerts caught her attention and held it. With her experience on the Lincoln papers as leverage, she established herself with the *Leader* as a part-time dramatic critic; and her reviews served double duty—she mailed them back to Lincoln, where her "Passing Show" column continued to run during the 1890s. A year after she had joined the *Home Monthly*, it was sold once more; and she moved to a full-time job with the *Leader* as assistant telegraph editor, which required routine editing of out-of-town news. Her daytime schedule left her free to attend the theater and to socialize, and her critical status broadened to encompass musical functions and book reviewing.

Although she found herself much in demand, with many men friends expressing an interest—a somewhat new and flattering turn—obviously Willa Cather never entertained any serious notion of marrying. Elizabeth Moorhead, who first met her in Pittsburgh in 1905, said that her first impression was that "here was a person who couldn't easily be diverted from her chosen course."⁴ A strong preference for remaining single, already apparent during Cather's university years, became a conscious decision in the prime marriageable time directly following her graduation. Her writing of that period—even her transitory reviews—speaks much of art and its stringent demands upon the individual who cares passionately; and her decision to be a writer merely strengthened with time. Marriage and a career in her thinking were incompatible. The dire consequences of acting as if they were otherwise are portrayed throughout her fiction, in which marriages for artists exist but are neither satisfying nor successful.

The circle of Cather friends, never large, was composed chiefly of those who shared her interests or who were themselves bent on artistic careers. Dorothy Canfield's father had moved to Ohio State University in Columbus; she visited Cather in Pittsburgh at intervals, and the friendship of these two young aspirants deepened. While working on *Home Monthly*, Cather met George Siebel, a young writer who had musical interests and whose cosmopolitan family was the kind toward which she gravitated whenever the opportunity arose. The Siebels, of German extraction but devotees of French literature, entertained her at their home on a weekly basis. Good home-cooked German food, good French readings in Gustave Flaubert, Victor Hugo, Théophile Gautier—who could want more? So much a family member did she become that she regularly spent her Christmases with them.

After serving her journalistic apprenticeship in Pittsburgh, Willa

Cather should have abandoned the steel city as soon as humanly possible. She told Latrobe Carroll in 1921 that she could never have learned so much about people and the world from her Pittsburgh years if she had been editing and writing; but it seems more probable that, had she proceeded at once to New York, her writing career might have blossomed sooner. But she stayed, probably because of a certain reserve, a measure of insecurity, and because life was made seductively pleasant by activities and friends. Even so, the reviewing of plays and concerts and books was not Willa Cather's major objective, and her own creative work crept ahead all too slowly. In 1898 and 1899, for instance, only two stories from her pen appeared in print; and she was in her mid-twenties when her production of mature work should have been prodigious. The next year's output was more promising: five stories appeared in the *Library*, a small, short-lived literary sheet. A national magazine, *Cosmopolitan*, accepted "Eric Hermannson's Soul," another effort of Cather's in mastering the story of Nebraska immigrant life on the Divide. Because she had so many pieces coming into print, she felt optimistic not only about her career but about the world itself. It seemed a good place to live in, she wrote her friend Will Owen Jones, and 1900 was shaping up as the happiest year of her life.[5]

II *Free Board at the McClungs'*

During the winter of 1900–01 Willa Cather attempted a break with Pittsburgh, but her translating for a government office in Washington was a mistake from the start. Not even extracurricular assignments—she sent news of the capital to papers in Lincoln and wrote a column for publication in Pittsburgh—made her work palatable. In February she wisely left Washington, but unwisely, she went not to New York but back to Pittsburgh. She may well have been influenced to return for the security offered by a new friend; Willa Cather had made the acquaintance in 1898 of Isabelle McClung, the beautiful daughter of a Pittsburgh judge.

The McClungs, independently wealthy, inhabited a world Cather had never known: their mansion was staffed by servants; their address was fashionable Murray Hill near the Monongahela; their gracious style of living included much leisure. The girls' mutual interest in the theater first drew them together—they met in an actress' dressing room—and a deep comradeship soon resulted in which Isabelle served as that individual "every writer needs most, the helping friend."[6] When the elder McClungs were persuaded by their daughter to invite Cather to stay at least temporarily in their spacious home, she accepted and lived with them for five years. Simultaneously, she gave up journalism to embark on another wrong track, teaching. As the spring semester began, she took a position at Pittsburgh's Central High School where she taught Latin at first (hard work because she had forgotten so much from her college days) and later, to her relief, English. There she stayed until 1905, when she shifted across the river to Allegheny High School.

The picture that emerges of Willa Cather in the years following 1900 is that of an eager and aspiring—but frustrated—young writer struggling for the courage to devote herself wholly to a literary career. As a result an almost unendurable tension was building. Being free of serious entanglements or responsibilities, having only herself to care for, and having achieved her break with the strong ties of Nebraska, Cather was free to go where and when she pleased. Yet she remained in Pittsburgh, bound to her teacher's desk, attempting to balance antagonistic careers. What held her back from taking the essential, all-or-nothing plunge into being a writer seems to have been a deep need for the security of her Pittsburgh situation and a lingering self-doubt that she possessed the ability to "make it" on the national scene. Her basic fear was mitigated only in part by her publications in prestige magazines such as *Cosmopolitan* and *Saturday Evening Post.*

At the McClungs' Cather was much too comfortable; everything possible was arranged to facilitate her career. The room she and Isabelle shared lay at the back of the house overlooking the garden and the slope leading to the Monongahela, a region of greenery, many trees, and no close neighbors to disturb their sense of privacy. For her writing an attic sewing room was transformed into a study where Cather, far from the bustle on the lower floors, could enjoy the solitude on which creativity thrives. On weekends particularly this refuge was crucially important, for Cather was committed to long hours five days a week, and she also had student themes to be graded.

Aside from an occasional free evening when neither a play nor a concert was scheduled, Saturdays and Sundays were the principal times that Cather could call her own. During these weekends no attention need be paid to anything but the stories and poems that teased her mind. Even Isabelle's Sunday afternoon literary teas were not allowed to intrude on Cather's privacy. The temptation to join the guests downstairs was powerful, since faculty members from Carnegie Tech's drama and music departments were often present, as well as members of the Dante society to which Isabelle belonged. But Cather, even though she was the central attraction at McClungs'—a kind of writer in residence—usually declined. "She would be at her desk in the attic leagues away . . . in that rich world of imagination," Elizabeth Moorhead reported; "Sunday afternoons should be kept for her own work. . . . she must let nothing interfere."[7]

To leave Pittsburgh meant a break with Isabelle McClung— a separation Willa Cather was loath to make. Always rather desperately in need of friends, she felt particularly close to Isabelle—so close that in 1916, when her friend announced her impending marriage, Cather found herself unable to start the new novel she had scheduled because of her fear that marriage would mean the death of their special relationship.[8] When Isabelle died in 1938, Cather told friends that she did not feel she could continue to exist,

III *Europe*

Since Willa Cather apparently was expected to make no contribution toward her room and board at the McClung home, her $650 annual salary stretched a long way, and she was able to use her savings to pay for her first trip abroad in 1902. With Isabelle as her companion, this voyage was an adventure long anticipated. The young women headed first for England, where they visited A. E. Housman in London; for Cather had developed great enthusiam for Housman after reading his "A Shropshire Lad." Since she had recently been devoting her own efforts to verse, this contact with her current favorite was important. When Dorothy Canfield joined them in London, they crossed the channel to France, landed at Dieppe, and then proceeded to Rouen, Paris, and southern France.

Halfway around the globe from Nebraska, France existed in Willa Cather's imagination as a totally new and strange world,—something altogether so different from anything she had known that she was amazed when she saw near Barbizon wheat fields that were "quite as level as those of the Nebraska divides." The power of a gale in the South, "more terrible than any wind that ever came up from Kansas," surprised her equally. Her notions of Nebraska's uniqueness needed revamping; the world was not after all so very different.

What impressed her even more than resemblances to home was the long unbroken panorama of history suggested at every step of the journey, the sense of civilization lovingly nurtured, and the opportunity for touching indirectly the lives of artists long admired: Flaubert, Maupassant, Daudet, and particularly Balzac, whose lingering presence in Paris made him seem to her infinitely "more a living fact than a dead man of letters."[9]

In Europe Willa Cather satisfied two needs; but neither was ever made explicit, and both were most likely unconscious. Her strong ties with things foreign, first established during her girlhood on the Divide, were revitalized when she saw for herself the lands from which her immigrants had sailed. At the same time everything she saw of the world at large brought her an improved perspective on her own native postage stamp of land. What Nebraska signified was more fully comprehended, and this understanding prepared her for a major expression of the state and its diverse peoples in her novels and stories.

These tales were not being written in 1902, and they were not to be written until Willa Cather herself forced a drastic change in the subordination of her writing to her full-time employment. At her age—she turned thirty in 1903—major works should have been underway, but her energy-draining classroom duties and the planned schedule of social life at McClungs were not helpful. Even so, a persistent urge to produce work of solidity and some magnitude was apparent. To be published in a magazine, as ephemeral almost as a newspaper appearance, no longer satisfied her. Something more concrete was demanded; something hefty to hold in the hands, carry about, set on a shelf; something with its own identity that would neither perish as suddenly as an actor's performance nor be buried among others' work in throwaway daily sheets. In short, she experienced an irresistible drive to write a book. And within three years of her return from Europe, she produced two.

IV   April Twilights

The various claims on Cather's time prevented the concentrated effort necessary to write a book-length work; however, a volume could be compiled through other means, and, not surprisingly, the first books to carry the Cather name were collections. She had been interested in writing verse since her college days, and poetry could be worked on in the brief hours available to her. The daily routine might even be advantageous, as it allowed her mind to toy with an idea even while her attention was actively engaged elsewhere. Then at day's end the lyric impulse could be released. In 1903 she collected a group of her poems under the title *April Twilights* and subsidized its publication by Richard Badger.

As poetry, Cather's book was not a great one, perhaps not even a genuinely promising one. As a step in her literary evolution, the book served its purpose; for *April Twilights*, with its impressive Boston imprint, brought her some measure of local fame and a degree of notice on a wider scale. At their worst the poems fell into wholly conventional lines indistinguishable from the verses of a host of aspirants to the thrones recently vacated by John Greenleaf Whittier, Henry Wadsworth Longfellow, William Cullen Bryant, and other dominant figures. Reflecting the current literary and artistic fashion, classical Greek and Roman themes predominate: "Antinous," "Winter at Delphi," "Lament for Marsyas," and "Paradox." Other poems, such as "London Roses" and "Poppies on Ludlow Castle," though lyrical attempts to respond to the European visit, slavishly imitate Housman:

> Lads and their sweethearts lying
> In the cleft of the windy hill;
> Hearts that are hushed of their sighing,
> Lips that are tender and still.[10]

The largest group of poems evokes nature in bursts of feeling; some, however finely drawn, remain traditional themes traditionally expressed. The lines "Winter lasts a five-month, / Spring-time stays but one" are quite representative.

Among all the twenty-four verses, only one poem in any way suggests the author of *O Pioneers!* and *My Ántonia*. In the briefest poem of all, one catches at last a glimpse of what was to come. In eight lines of blank verse, "Prairie Dawn" establishes a clear link with the Nebraska experience:

> A crimson fire that vanquishes the stars;
> A pungent odor from the dusty sage;
> A sudden stirring of the huddled herds;
> A breaking of the distant table-lands
> Through purple mists ascending, and the flare
> Of water-ditches silver in the light;

A swift, bright lance hurled low across the world;
A sudden sickness for the hills of home.[11]

Willa Cather's successful verses were invariably inspired by western
themes and composed in free forms. In her best—"The Swedish
Mother," "Prairie Spring," "Macon Prairie," "Going Home"—she
managed the same freedom from artificiality that quickened her
major stories. The resultant poem was spontaneous, economical,
and concrete—a pouring out of memories deeply treasured.

April Twilights announced that American poets, few as they were
in 1903, had little to fear in the way of competition. Later, her fame
as a novelist solidly established, Willa Cather herself said quite
candidly, "I do not take myself seriously as a poet." Critical agreement was almost unanimous.[12]

V   The Troll Garden

Willa Cather's second book—also a collection—was more por-
tentous, a book of stories issued under an obscurely allusive title,
The Troll Garden, with epigraphs from Christina Rosetti and
Charles Kingsley.[13] Among its seven tales are examples of the short
story rarely surpassed either by Cather herself or by other Americans. This fact might not be immediately apparent, for the gems of
this collection are scattered among trivialities. Cather was riding the
crest of a grand passion for the work of Henry James, in her opinion
"the perfect writer";[14] and since the 1890s she had been influenced
by his stories of artists, their dedication, their tribulations, and their
rewards. She admired these tales particularly for their excellence of
style and form; consequently, the bulk of her *Troll Garden* stories
concerned artists.

Three stories, far superior to the others, forecast Cather's mature
work. "Paul's Case," which approaches the question of artistry from
the viewpoint of a boy utterly without talent but hopelessly deluded
into believing he can nourish himself through life as a hanger-on, is
by all odds the superior story in the group. A finished product, it is
genuine in its approach and in its clean, simple prose. It became
Cather's most anthologized selection; it was in fact for a time the
only story she would allow to be republished. Two others, only
slightly less successful, owe their existence directly to her Nebraska
years; both "A Wagner Matinée" and "The Sculptor's Funeral" confront the impossibility of artistic fulfillment on a frontier where
practical needs are overwhelming. These stories project Cather's

fundamental problem in her postuniversity years: the tension between the need to support herself and the deep urge to dedicate her
life to art.

"It is always hard to write about the things that are near your
heart," Willa Cather admitted some years after publishing *The Troll
Garden*. "From a kind of instinct of self-protection you distort and
disguise them."[15] The masked concerns in "Paul's Case," "A Wagner Matinée," and "The Sculptor's Funeral" are revealed even in
summaries of the stories. A boy is doomed to be a mere observer of
artists, never to approach closer than the window glass through
which he participates vicariously in their careers. An old woman,
beaten by life on the Divide, faces the bitter fact that her Boston
visit, with its concerts, must give way to a return to the frontier;
having spent her life in other, more immediate pursuits, her day has
passed by. A sculptor dies just as his career gets under way; and he
is buried by townspeople who lack even the most elementary understanding of his work—people who, if they did understand, would
be incapable of caring. None of these stories is necessarily that of
Willa Cather herself; but beneath their surfaces run, like currents in
the sea, Cather's own impelling terrors: that she may lack the major
talent essential to transform ambition into achievement; that the
lure of family, the security of a salary might distract her from her
goal; that youth might pass without having been fully utilized.

VI *Life under the Volcano*

By 1903 Willa Cather had composed the stories in *The Troll
Garden* and was long overdue for her break with Pittsburgh. Her
debilitating teaching responsibilities and the luxurious diversions
supplied by the McClungs, whether she could recognize the fact or
not, had become liabilities. Unable in any manner to advance her
career, they were distractions that held her back from what was hers
to achieve. But she seemed in a state of psychological paralysis that
prevented her from breaking with established routine. However, a
"fortunate accident" occurred—a chain of circumstances that
brought her work to the attention of S. S. McClure, the publisher of
America's fastest growing magazine. *McClure's* rocketing circulation
had been stimulated by aggressive muckraking articles produced by
a stable of crusading journalist-authors that included Ida Tarbell,
Lincoln Steffens, and Ray Stannard Baker. McClure was ever on the
lookout for promising writers, for his nature would not allow him to

sit waiting for manuscripts to drift in via the postman. Hearing Cather's work praised, he promptly wrote her a personal note inviting her to submit for consideration any stories she might have on hand. Thrilled—shocked also, most likely—to receive unsolicited encouragement from one of the brightest lights in publishing, Cather responded with her recently completed tales; and McClure, who was prone to sudden enthusiasms, saw at once a very real possibility for a collection

McClure telegraphed Cather in Pittsburgh to propose an interview in New York. His biographer, Peter Lyon, has suggested the type of encounter she must have experienced in the magazine's offices. McClure, with his way of overwhelming new acquaintances, would have done most of the talking; but his conversation would have sparkled with "an exhilarating account of affairs in the great world" of publishing and with a sprinkling of references to his dealings with literary figures whose names Cather would recognize. It would, in fact, be a monologue; McClure's rush of talk would catch Cather up like a leaf in a whirlwind—but she was a willing leaf.[16]

Willa Cather's own account of the interview indicates that this is precisely the way it went, and it is fair to say that her encounter with McClure caused an instantaneous change in her life. Recognizing this fact, she lost no time in writing to Lincoln to inform Will Owen Jones, who had been instrumental in acquainting McClure with her potentialities. Jones would be happy to know that he had succeeded in his efforts to launch the Cather career, for since her two-hour interview in New York, life had become a totally new proposition. She had walked into the *McClure's* building feeling that she was not anything of particularly great value, but when she came out, she knew that her worth had soared. The clue was in her attitude toward the streetcars; where previously she had paid them little heed, now she took extra caution lest one strike her and end a life so greatly worth saving.[17]

The personality of McClure himself worked this miraculous change—Cather was certain of it. Something about his boyish enthusiasm gripped her attention so firmly as to convert her instantly to his way of thinking. She felt positive that if he had been propagandizing for a religious view, she would have become an instant convert. His charisma was powerful. He was a man for whose sake followers would willingly be burned at the stake. McClure won Willa Cather's heart during their first interview by his actions when he learned that some of her fiction had been rejected by his magazine; calling the readers to his office, he demanded that they account for their stewardship. For Cather this was a glorious moment. A spectator, she sat watching the confrontation, her chin held high, and thought her hour had struck. McClure took the stories, and to her surprise he did not require a single change. He fairly brimmed with plans to make something important of her.[18]

A volume would come eventually, but first McClure planned magazine publication—good for circulation, good for boosting a new reputation. With his usual acumen he reserved the finest of the stories, "Paul's Case" and "The Sculptor's Funeral," for *McClure's;* and he placed the next best, "A Wagner Matinée," in *Everybody's,* his chief rival in the muckraking genre. *Scribner's* published "A Death in the Desert."

McClure was without a doubt not only one of the editorial geniuses of his day but also a man of high volatility. The fireworks atmosphere he created was exhausting to his staff, but none ever doubted his sensational fecundity. If McClure, mind spinning like a top, could toss off twenty large ideas in a week, all but one or two were certain to be impractical or downright fantastic.[19] "Asking S. S. McClure for ideas," said Will Irwin, "was like praying for rain in the Amazon jungle." Those who worked with him left no end of anecdotes, and praise went hand in hand with accounts of somewhat less lovable qualities. *Variable, temperamental, extravagant* are the adjectives that Lincoln Steffens felt best described his employer; and *unorganizable, impatient, disorderly* are the tags added by Ray Stannard Baker, who regarded McClure as "all intuition and impulse" and who was astounded at the man's melodramatic methods for impressing his editors. Consistency was not one of his virtues; today's favorite scheme might be discarded tomorrow and the "greatest editorial idea ever conceived" might take its place. Impetuosity was hard on a magazine staff who had monthly deadlines to meet. Somehow the editors had to make distinctions on a realistic basis and follow productive leads. There were articles and entire series to be developed.[20]

McClure so erupted with ideas that he reminded Ray Stannard Baker of a live volcano. Too excitable ever to stand still, he was forever rushing off on field trips, seeking new subjects, searching for new writers. These forays, which might take him to outposts of the Far West or across the Atlantic to Europe and Africa, produced heaps of manuscripts and scores of major plans. In his absence McClure's staff could proceed with some equanimity to edit the magazine until the calm was broken by the boss's return. To the staff's mingled joy and despair, "He would come straight from the ship to the office," said Steffens, "call us together, and tell us what he had seen and heard, said and done. With his valise full of clippings, papers, books and letters, to prove it, he showed us that he had the greatest features any publisher ever had, the most marvelous, really world-stunning ideas or stories."[21] And McClure often had really found such stories: Rudyard Kipling's *Kim*, for one, was acquired in this way.

Ida Tarbell, who participated in such "endless excited staff meetings," placed considerable value on them: "I had come to look upon Mr. McClure's returns as the most genuinely creative moments of our magazine life. He was an extraordinary reporter; his sense of the meaning, the meat of a man or event, his vivid imagination, his necessity of discharging on the group at once, before they were cold, his observations, intuitions, ideas, experiences, made the gatherings on his return amazingly stimulating to me."[22]

Trouble brewed seasonally in the magazine's offices for, despite genuine admiration for the publisher, his associates chafed against his variability and his constant insistence that his writers pursue his ideas as he produced them. "He wanted the fun," said Ida Tarbell understandingly, "of seeing his finds quickly in print." At times he seemed in his impatience to be oblivious to the need for rigorous checking, research, and documentation. According to Steffens he ran a dictatorship, albeit a benevolent one; "he could raise a rumpus" when thwarted by his employees.[23] As tensions heightened, the underlings could raise a rumpus themselves; although most of them had come to the magazine relatively unknown and had built considerable reputations under the publisher's tutelage, they grew independent as their names became prominent, their readers more numerous, and their services in greater demand.

McClure could scarcely hope to hold the lid on this boiling pot. Inevitably there was a shake up. Intraoffice politics became bitter; the staff considered leaving the magazine and starting one of their own. Eventually John S. Phillips, of McClure, Phillips and Company, laid before them a plan to purchase the *American Magazine*. Tarbell, Baker, Steffens, and others resigned in a wholesale "desertion" that precipitated a crisis. With the backbone of his staff broken, McClure had to form a new group at once or perish. He entertained no doubts of his ability to find suitable replacements. With another bunch of raw but talented recruits, he was certain he could work the same miracle again.

As he searched for capable individuals presently unattached or otherwise susceptible to being drawn into his fold, it was quite natural that the name of his schoolteacher-writer from Pittsburgh should be recalled. Overnight Willa Cather found herself in receipt of an astounding offer: would she leave Pittsburgh to go work for McClure in New York? To make certain that she accepted, S. S. McClure himself, like "a far-off benignant deity, descended in the flesh upon Pittsburgh."[24] He came to dinner at Judge McClung's house; and, his blue eyes flashing, he dominated the table talk with his adventures in the writing world. He seemed determined to carry Willa Cather away with him, and he did so. For her it was the opportunity of a lifetime.

Because the offer arrived in May, in only a matter of days Cather could accept. The school year ended; then it was off to New York to be swept into the roaring current known as *McClure's*. Cather was blessed with remarkable self-assurance, but she must have wondered what had possessed this great editor to select her. The famous McClure intuition was not inconsiderable; but, to all intents and purposes, he seemed to be employing someone "almost totally unknown and untested."[25]

In 1905 Cather had spent a week as McClure's guest in New York; "now here she was again, obedient to his summons, but a little uncertain as to what was expected of her."[26] What was expected soon became clear; she was to take hold immediately and transform herself into the professional editor writer he decreed her to be. Most of the staff were neophytes like herself: Will Irwin; Cameron Mackenzie, then only twenty-four; and Ellery Sedgwick, later the famous long-time editor of *Atlantic Monthly*. But the energetic Mr. McClure was always there to teach them; and by working harder than anyone else, he set the example for all: in the morning he was in his office by 8:30. When midnight came, he might well be hard at work yet.

As before, only when he dashed off on one of his out-of-town scouting trips were his new editors able to act independently, to have the responsibility for the magazine, and to find the time to pursue their specialities. Also as before, not all took kindly to the

McClure routine. Because some were unable to work with a tornado in their midst, *McClure's* continued to undergo periodic upheavals; however, Willa Cather always remained. Eternally grateful to her "boss," she repaid him with the full measure of her literary judgment, with hard work, and with absolute fidelity. Her loyalty kept her with the magazine long past the time she should have stayed; *McClure's*, like Pittsburgh, became mere ballast holding her down.

But in the beginning she had much to learn from McClure himself. He held definite ideas of an editor's duties, and an editor soon understood that creative editing was done only in the field, never at a desk in a comfortable room. Ida Tarbell had learned this from him, as had Lincoln Steffens. Informed that he would never learn to edit a magazine in the New York office and asking where then he should go, Steffens was told, "Anywhere. Anywhere else. Get out of here, travel, go—somewhere. . . . Buy a railroad ticket, get on a train, and there, where it lands you, you will learn to edit a magazine."[27]

In all likelihood Willa Cather was told the same thing; but, in any event, she learned McClure did not expect her to stay put in the office. After her orientation had been accomplished, he put an important assignment into her hands and gave her a railroad ticket. In his search for items to tickle the public palate—controversial if possible, and the more outré, the better—McClure had chanced upon a lengthy manuscript by Mrs. Georgine Milmine. It was not the most perfect manuscript in the world, but its subject matter—Mrs. Mary Baker Eddy and her Christian Science movement—seemed surefire. Milmine's provocative but slipshod book was being readied for use as a major serial; and accuracy, of course, was indispensable since *McClure's* reputation was grounded upon dependable facts. It handled red-hot issues, and it presented them incontrovertibly. But a number of errors had been detected already in the Milmine manuscript, and these were unthinkable when they occurred on a sensitive issue. The only solution was for trustworthy Willa Cather to take the manuscript in hand. By this time McClure relied on the sanity of her judgments; he could count on her to be thorough in checking the facts. But she had to work on location at the center of the Christian Science movement, and doing so meant traveling to Boston for as long a stay as the job might require.

VII   *House of Memories*

Not long after her arrival in Boston in 1908, Willa Cather was invited to visit the widow of the famous publisher James T. Fields at her home—one of the truly momentous visits of her life. Annie Fields, then past seventy but most definitely "not old" in mind or spirit, lived at 148 Charles Street. In her time Charles Dickens, William Makepeace Thackeray, and Matthew Arnold had been her house guests; and James Russell Lowell and Oliver Wendell Holmes were regularly entertained by her. Ticknor and Fields, the publishing house, itself held a significance for Cather, who had not forgotten her father's bookcase in Red Cloud and its "little volumes of Longfellow and Hawthorne with that imprint."[28]

A sense of living history permeated the Fields drawing room, for its hostess herself seemed miraculously to "reach back to Waterloo." From her personal recollections Mrs. Fields could speak of Cather's idol, Henry James, and of his earliest efforts at composition; of Robert and Elizabeth Browning and their life in Italy; of her dinner party in Dickens' honor at which Dr. Oliver Wendell Holmes had spoken of actors "in a way that quite disturbed Longfellow." On every hand "that house of memories," as Cather remembered it, was stocked with mementos. One day Annie Fields might display a lock of John Keats' hair given her by the painter Joseph Severn; on the next she might show Cather cabinets stuffed with manuscripts from pretypewriter times and open them so that her new friend could examine the pristine handwriting that even the printers had taken care not to smudge. The house was more than a mere sanctuary from a too rapidly changing world; for if Mrs. Fields introduced Cather to the poems of John Donne and sent her home with two fat volumes to savor, she also introduced her to a living writer who became a decisive influence on her career.[29]

So it was not Mrs. Fields who became the central attraction on that first afternoon at 148 Charles Street but Sarah Orne Jewett, who was a guest the day Cather visited. In 1908 the author of *Deephaven, The Country of the Pointed Firs,* and other stories about Maine and its people stood in the first ranks of the local-color realists. Cather's image of her had been formed through playing the childhood game of Authors, in which the players attempt to match in pairs cards of a deck printed with portraits of novelists and poets. She at once recognized Miss Jewett, even though she had grown stout and grey. Suddenly the mementos, keepsakes, and manuscripts that Cather had come to examine meant very little to her.

From these two significant women Willa Cather could learn much. However different she might be from the immigrant women on the Divide, Mrs. Fields seemed, like them, to be a model of fortitude, of genuine ability, and of a fine, intelligent approach to living; she reinforced lessons learned in Nebraska twenty years before. From Miss Jewett, Willa could learn the secrets of her chosen profession. She had long recognized that Sarah Orne Jewett offered something quite apart from the depressing round of "machine-made historical novels" and "dreary dialect stories" that dominated contemporary writing. Her work probed deeper than the heavy, superficial works of popular authors like John Fox, Jr., whose books dominated the bestseller lists; indeed his *The Trail of the Lonesome Pine* at that moment was well on the way toward totaling a sale for the decade of seven hundred and fifty thousand copies.[30]

In Miss Jewett, Willa Cather also recognized a writer of unimpeachable integrity who concentrated her efforts on the region she knew most intimately, who refused to strive unduly for flashy effects, and who, rather than concocting a trumped-up pseudo-dialect to humor her readers, used her native idiom, "the finest language any writer can have." Above all, Miss Jewett's own personality impressed itself on every page of her work; as Cather recognized, "[Miss Jewett] had with her own stories and her own characters a very charming relation, spirited, gay, tactful, noble in its essence and a little arch in its expression." It was refreshing and reassuring for Cather to meet a writer unimpressed by the merely fashionable, one not deterred by the noisily publicized "masterpieces" that in any given month or year spewed from the presses "like trunks pouring down the baggage chutes from an overcrowded ocean steamer."[31]

Miss Jewett responded to Willa Cather with the gift of friendship, and they enjoyed at the Fields' many talks, usually about literature. During one of these the two were commenting upon a recent magazine story about a mule; the story's claim to fame appeared to center on the fact that its rural author had been simply and solely a mule driver. The story itself struck both women as hopelessly limited, parochial, and ungrammatical; and Miss Jewett summarized: "You must know the world before you can know the village."[32] These words struck a chord in that they seemed full of wisdom to Cather, although Miss Jewett was not prone to making "wise" pronouncements. Committing the remark to memory, Cather quoted it often; and she more importantly applied it to herself and to her attitude toward the youthful materials that soon emerged as ideas for her novels. Her years away from Nebraska, and everything she saw and heard in Pittsburgh, New York, Europe, and Boston were contributing toward her broader perspective about the flat lands of home. Miss Jewett caused her to see more clearly what she was accomplishing by her flight from the Divide. One must step off into the distance, Miss Jewett seemed to advise, in order to fit properly one's own tiny corner of the world into the universal scheme.

The Cather-Jewett friendship lasted only a brief sixteen months, for the older writer, ill when they met, died the following year. After Cather's assignment in Boston had been completed, the two corresponded regularly; and in one of her notes Miss Jewett included the second sentence that became axiomatic to Cather: "The thing that teases the mind over and over for years, and at last gets itself put down rightly on paper—whether little or great, it belongs to Literature."[33] This statement defined to Cather the creative process on its highest level; if it did not alter her course in life, it surely buttressed notions she had already approached intuitively. There were youthful materials—scenes, characters, anecdotes, themes— that since her university days she had been attempting to record *rightly*. Her efforts to date seemed shamefully experimental, amateurish, and awkward; but with a volition of their own, these same memories persisted in urging themselves as subjects: life on the Nebraska Divide, the struggle of the gifted individual to achieve.

VIII *Toward a First First-Novel*

As Willa Cather's tenure at *McClure's* lengthened into years, her responsibilities smothered her own writing. She produced assigned pieces for the magazine: major articles on the arts and summary reviews of the drama, opera, and ballet seasons. There was the Mary Baker Eddy series and book, which was only nominally by Georgine Milmine after Cather had reworked it. In addition, S. S. McClure, who in 1907 had turned fifty, wished to publish the story of his rags-to-riches life. Always an idea man rather than a writer, he prevailed upon his managing editor to ghost his autobiography; and Willa Cather, grateful to the man—now a friend—who had brought her from a high-school classroom to the forefront of American journalism, could not decline. Because of her genuine affection for him, the assignment became a labor of love, and no author credit was

involved. But McClure, both in the magazine serialization and in
book form, preceded his story with a special acknowledgement of
his debt to Cather.[34]

By 1912, which marked the sixth year of Cather's editorship, the
thrill of connection with a leading magazine had dimmed; the excitement of a first plunge into the metropolitan center had given
way to more sober reflection. Cather had solidified new friendships
with Edith Lewis and Elizabeth Shepley Sergeant, both of whom
after her death wrote memoirs of her. She attended the opera regularly, she had satisfied her thirst for good theater, and she had been
introduced to notable after notable. She had traveled extensively,
home to Red Cloud as usual, and to Pittsburgh; to England in 1908
with Isabelle, again in 1909 for *McClure's*. But none of this experience sufficed for what was missing: whatever she was doing seemed
second best and not what she was ultimately intended to do.

In making a final break with the magazine, her resolve was
strengthened, indeed shaped, by Sarah Orne Jewett in a unique
series of letters that offered advice. The older writer, without ever
needing to state the obvious, had adopted Willa Cather as a protégée; and in her last months she shared the wisdom she had accumulated and gently guided Cather toward goals that seemed important. Having read "On the Gull's Road," a story that Cather had
given *McClure's*, she praised it in a letter that also cautioned her
against the use of the masculine viewpoint that was so difficult for a
woman to achieve; moreover, for one sex to counterfeit the other
always smacked of contrivance. What Miss Jewett liked about "On
the Gull's Road" was less important than what the story might portend: "It makes me the more sure that you are far on your road
toward a fine and long story of very high class." The gentle nudge
toward the novel form comes through clearly if subliminally. In *The
Troll Garden*, "The Sculptor's Funeral" marked the highest
achievement, Miss Jewett felt; and more in that vein was indicated:
"You have your Nebraska life," an asset of incalculable value, she
reminded Cather. Yet perspective was needed on the Cather
backgrounds, which appeared to be seen too much from within.
Cather must "guard and mature" her force and then pour her best
into what had been selected for treatment. There could be no compromise on quality, no patience with the thin or the cheap: "We
must know it *is* cheapness and not make believe about it."[35]

To be engaged in ghost writing, even for a friend such as

McClure, or to be put to researching and revising the inaccurate documents of others was a waste of a talent such as Cather's. It squandered something unique, and its results would be destructive. Miss Jewett approached the topic diplomatically: "I cannot help saying what I think about your writing and its being hindered by such incessant, important, responsible work as you have in your hands now," she wrote, evidently in specific reference to the Milmine manuscript. But the crucial thing to consider was whether hack work could be allowed to continue if Cather's own creative abilities were ever to mature. The big question the younger writer had to ask herself was whether five years hence she might be writing things finer in any way than she was writing now: "This you are anxiously saying to yourself." And Willa Cather was undoubtedly asking this question, for she knew. she possessed something uncommon. The simple act of reading through piles of unimaginative manuscripts submitted to *McClure's* was enough to demonstrate the superiority of her own talent.[36]

Before her death Miss Jewett wrote about the hazards involved in balancing a personal writing career with a full-time job in editing. "I think it is impossible," she concluded. In competition against the magazine's incessant demands on time and energy, the artist was bound to lose. "Your vivid, exciting companionship in the office," she warned, "must not be your audience, you must find your own quiet centre of life, and write from that to the world." Cather cherished this letter; for in stating baldly what she already sensed about herself, it made her painfully aware that her publishing day was comparable only with the exhausting gyrations of a trapeze act.[37]

Tactfully Miss Jewett suggested that Cather was approaching the middle years without having produced work of substantial scope. "When one's first working power has spent itself," she cautioned, "nothing ever brings it back." Willa was asked to consider a more specific instance—to suppose that 1908, rather than having been spent in Boston and in long office hours bringing order to the Milmine articles,—had gone into "three or four stories" of the caliber of "The Sculptor's Funeral." This speculation Willa Cather could not dismiss.[38]

In 1911, after procrastinating for too long, she prepared to ease out of *McClure's* and to drive toward that "quiet centre" that Miss Jewett had prescribed. Early in that year she was stricken with mastoiditis, and she must have emerged from her hospitalization and recuperation, which took months, more aware than ever of life's precarious quality and convinced that, if she ever were going to devote her talents fully to the things that teased her mind, she must soon do so. To wait much longer might be fatal to her artistic hopes. Her weeks of illness and her separation from the office environment had provided some perspective on the editorial life and set her mind free to think about more significant things—the most urgent being her suppressed urge to write only on her own subjects. "Dream your dreams," Sarah Orne Jewett had advised.

In June, during her recuperation, Willa Cather went to Miss Jewett's girlhood home in South Berwick, Maine, and found it, as she had hoped, the one spot on earth where she could gain a perfect rest. Maine was a fine, isolated spot in which to achieve a perspective on her career. Elizabeth Sergeant, who had obtained a copy of *The Troll Garden*, wrote to say how much she liked the stories. Cather replied that not much in these tales seemed truly good to her now—not even in the Nebraska stories, which she thought marred by a petulant viewpoint she had not been able to refrain from expressing in those youthful days when she had felt chained unfairly to the West and barred from all the things she really wanted to do and when she had feared it really might be her destiny to die in a cornfield. But South Berwick was a long distance from Nebraska, and a long way from *McClure's;* here, in house and grounds alike, Miss Jewett's influence seemed still to be a living presence. In her imagination Cather thought it not impossible to encounter her friend's spirit as she strolled down the garden paths; she was certain that if such a meeting did occur, Miss Jewett's ghost would brood over the loss of elegance suffered by the world in recent years. Cather, fresh from the battle of machines and men that now characterized New York for her, understood what loss it was that would trouble her mentor.[39] But in Miss Jewett's garden it was possible to forget, temporarily, much that was depressing: the pervasive banality of so much modern fiction, such as Mr. Rex Beach's novels, and the unending flood of articles on sensational topics like white slavery, which were the mainstay of the journalistic exposé. In South Berwick Cather could see plainly that the overwhelming vulgarity of the magazine world was light years removed from what she must do with her life. She understood that a change must occur, for Art's claim to a wholehearted commitment could no longer be denied.[40]

Willa Cather's other commitment, to Mr. McClure, brought her back to New York and to her magazine editing, but she returned with grave misgivings and remained only briefly. As fall began, she took a leave of absence, accompanying Isabelle McClung to Cherry Valley in the Finger Lakes area of New York, where the two rented a house. In this rural setting of hills, quiet waters, and autumn maples, peaceful with the summer people departed, Cather at last was free to work; and she wrote unstintingly. During her illness she had created a book-length work and had composed it during the following summer. Her first order of business at Cherry Valley was to complete this story and to arrange for its serialization in *McClure's* the following spring. It was, as she later referred to it, her first "first novel"; and since she still idolized Henry James as the commanding personage in American letters, *Alexander's Bridge* is highly Jamesian in its symmetry of form and its engrossing interest in relationships between people of an artistic bent. Through Ferris Greenslet, her friend since their meeting during her visit to Boston, she managed to schedule book publication by his firm, Houghton Mifflin.

Gathering momentum, Cather composed another story, "The Bohemian Girl," which was not much shorter than some of her later novels and which was scheduled to appear in *McClure's* not long after her novel ended its serialization. "The Bohemian Girl" was of an entirely different stamp from her novel, which was set in London for the most part and concerned artists. The first sentences of these two works might be compared profitably. *Alexander's Bridge* opens in Boston with Professor Lucius Wilson standing "at the head of Chestnut Street, looking about him with the pleased air of a man of taste," but "The Bohemian Girl" opens on a train: "The transcontinental express swung along the windings of the Sand River Valley, and in the rear seat of the observation car a young man sat greatly at his ease, not in the least discomfited by the fierce sunlight which beat in upon his brown face and neck and strong back."[41]

Nils Ericson's return to the Divide is quite literally Willa Cather's; her surrender to her more natural materials continued in another long tale of the Divide that she began at once and that opened on a day in the early 1880s among a "cluster of low drab buildings huddled on the gray prairie, under a gray sky." Based upon her reminiscences of the pioneers, this story was called "Alexandra." Not published at once, it served instead as the opening sequence of a longer work, *O Pioneers!*, which she referred to as her second first-novel because it placed her in the mainstream of her western materials.

Breaking with *McClure's* was not easy, and for most of another year Cather continued a tenuous relationship with the staff. But the threads holding her were progressively weakened; a month here, a month there, her time was less frequently given to her editorship. The final separation was eased by the unseating of S. S. McClure himself in another of the magazine's upheavals, and Cather no longer had any personal obligation to the firm. By 1913 Cather, now on her own, was determined to sink or to swim as a professional novelist; and never again did she plan to commit herself to an employee status if she could possibly avoid it. The intensity of her dedication, the force of her personal determination to put her writing first, last, and always, became legendary. Given the history of her activities in the two decades following university, it is also fully understandable. She was engaged in her search for perfection; nothing less would satisfy her. And to her this endeavor seemed worth whatever sacrifice might be demanded.

Of the many anecdotes suggestive of the nunlike vow Willa Cather took for her art, one of the most pointed comes from the recollections of Elizabeth Moorhead. She was well acquainted with the Cather aloofness, which was particularly rigid when a new book was in the making; and she fully understood why the writer was reluctant to spare so much as a moment for anything else during her creative sessions. But having a pair of tickets for the opera *Tristan* and knowing Cather's love for musical plays, she on a whim telephoned her friend and invited her. Willa Cather's reply, succinct and final, came without hesitation: "If you had two tickets for heaven, I wouldn't go!" [42]

IX   *A Wasted Decade*

Cather's careers in schoolteaching and journalism provided little material for her fiction. Here and there, as in "Uncle Valentine," a story might be set in Pittsburgh, but that background was never an indispensable one. "Paul's Case" does make some use of the classroom experience as background, and in *Alexander's Bridge* and *The Professor's House* her knowledge of teachers proved of some minor value; but teaching never became a rich fictional lode. Sarah Orne Jewett had felt certain that her protégée could make good use of

"the 'Bohemia' of newspaper and magazine-office life" in her writing
and had suggested it, along with the Nebraska years and the Virginia
childhood, as one of the three major backgrounds from which
Cather might draw. But Cather's long associations with newspapers
and with *McClure's* figure hardly at all in her major work.

Only one story is set in the offices of a great Muckraker magazine,
and "Ardessa" (1918) tells of a woman "not young and . . . certainly
not handsome" who works as special assistant to a Mr. O'Mally,
publisher of a "red-hot magazine of protest, which he called 'The
Outcry,' " built through his own imaginative energy. The Cather-
McClure-*McClure's* allusions are transparent, as are the methods
by which O'Mally is said to have developed his editor-writers: "On
his staff there were five famous men, and he had made every one of
them. At first it amused him to manufacture celebrities. He found
he could take an average reporter from the daily press, give him a
'line' to follow, a trust to fight, a vice to expose . . . and in two years
the reporter would be recognized as an authority."[43]

The creation of Muckrakers of the Tarbell-Steffens stamp comes
to mind; and Ardessa Devine thinks of her famous associates on *The
Outcry* as Cather must have considered the great names at
McClure's: "all about her, as contemplative as Buddhas in their
private offices, each meditating upon the particular trust or form of
vice confided to his care."[44] The sense of whirlwind activity at
McClure's and of Cather's own indispensability and entrapment are
evoked. Aside from its portrait of this milieu, however, "Ardessa,"
with its lightweight plot, is merely a concoction for putting the
background to fictional use; and the story demonstrates that her
McClure's years, stimulating as they may have been, were not Willa
Cather's natural material. With "Ardessa" she evidently cleared the
world of journalism from her system because she never, in her full
career, returned to it again.

X *New Literary Materials*

The years she spent in journalism may have been of small literary
value to Willa Cather, but a few months spent in the Southwest
provided her with indispensable materials. In the spring of 1912,
with *Alexander's Bridge* running serially in *McClure's* and the publication of "The Bohemian Girl" arranged, Cather went by train to
Arizona, where her brother Douglass worked for the Santa Fe. The
Southwest had always held an attraction for her, for its proximity to

Nebraska made it and its history a part of her general awareness; and even before her first visit to the area, she had written "The Enchanted Bluff," with its image of the mesa as a sacred and mysterious goal.

Cather had gone to Europe as a homecoming of sorts, a return to the lands of her forebears and her immigrants; and her trips abroad brought her a quiet and serene fulfillment. In contrast, the American Southwest captured her imagination as no land had ever captured it. This effect had roots in her childhood feeling that, in coming to Nebraska, she had wandered perilously close to the edge of the world. Whenever she was gone away from the West, she experienced an appetite to return that manifested itself physically, as a taste in the mouth, a remembered tang on the tongue. Yet Cather was unable to travel West without a mounting apprehension of impending loss. Just what she was doomed to lose, she could not say, but her feeling was similar to that of a nonswimmer who fights the water irrationally when dropped into it. She had the same urge to struggle whenever she was deposited in the West; unable to relax fully, she felt compelled to fight the current. For a long while Cather's chief fear was that she would never get out of Nebraska, that she would, as she put it, die in a cornfield; as a consequence, whenever she was in the West, she wanted to know precisely where she was and where the "exits" were located. This tension was uncomfortable, but it had the advantage of increasing her responsiveness to things around her, of making her more alert; and in the Southwest she found much to respond to.[45]

Not everything in Arizona was immediately attractive. The desert itself was not so bad—dull red in color and dry, like the dust from bricks; unending stretches of rabbitbrush and sage. But Douglass Cather was headquartered in the town of Winslow, which impressed his sister an an ugly, desolate, little place with practically nothing to recommend it to a visitor. Its bare grounds were strewn with trash—empty tin cans and wornout shoes seemed to predominate—and apparently it was populated entirely with dull railroad people. Willa came to Arizona in search of what should be the easiest thing to locate but which actually is the most elusive: four walls within which one can write with ease. She was not asking for a palace; but the houses, or "casas," of Winslow were tiny shacks, thin as eggshells, and even though Douglass was in charge of an entire "casa," Willa knew at once that the Winslow atmosphere was all wrong. Even if she could have written there otherwise, she felt she would have been prevented from doing so by the constant sand storms, some of which were powerful enough to stop the trains.[46]

So far as Willa Cather was concerned, this isolated desert town possessed only two redeeming features. One was a good hotel with a fine restaurant, an anomaly explained by the absence of dining cars on the Santa Fe, so that any through train arriving in Winslow near a meal time was certain to stop. The town's second advantage was its proximity to other localities served by the railroad; if one could not bear to stay in town, it was no trick at all to board the train and travel elsewhere. One such spot Willa had in mind was New Mexico, which she had traversed on her journey West. She was certain she could work easily there, especially in Albuquerque, which was situated in the loveliest countryside she had ever seen. More brilliant even than the area around Marseilles, this land was filled with Indian villages, not built as tourist traps, but genuine communities, each clustered close about its church. Other villages, dead now, had been Spanish missions at the time of Elizabeth I. In New Mexico God seemed to have set a splendid stage, Cather thought, not for motor cars and phonographs but for some great action—an immense tragedy or a new religion, something to equal the grandeur of the crusades. Between Trinidad and Alburquerque the country surpassed the valley of the Rhone in its beauty, she felt, while from Trinidad to Las Vegas the landscape was one unending purple mountain range.[47]

To Elizabeth Sergeant, recently ill in North Carolina, Cather wrote that she expected Douglass would take her to Albuquerque for a few days where she would inquire about a room for her friend to live and work in while recuperating. Cather herself, only a night away by train, would then plan to visit her, but she was confident that the city, with its attractive Spanish air, would act as a curative. Rather than visit Albuquerque, however, Douglass had plans to take his sister north, and on April 26 Willa informed Elizabeth Sergeant that Flagstaff and the cliff dwellers were to be their destination. At this time Cather apparently knew little of southwestern history, at least not enough to prepare her adequately for the breathtaking revelations that came to her in the next few days and that forever revised her opinion of the area.[48]

In Walnut Canyon, not far from Flagstaff, Willa Cather looked upon cliff dwellings for the first time. She had heard of them, of course, but had never before encountered them; and they had a galvanic effect upon her, particularly as observed in their native ambience and in a context of hiking, horseback riding, and cliff scaling. From Flagstaff Cather went on to the Grand Canyon and a series of dawn-to-dusk excursions in a horse-drawn wagon; then she and Douglass planned a further trip along the Little Colorado river to look on their own for other cliff dwellings. Her discovery of this ancient culture came in time to be woven into *The Song of the Lark;* although three years away from publication, that novel was already shaping up in Cather's mind. In the novel Thea Kronborg, quite like Cather herself, retires to Arizona to recuperate from illness; she requires a change from steady work and faces an important career decision. What Thea happens upon in Panther Canyon (Cather's pseudonym for Walnut Canyon) is the ordered life of the past. The experience begins in a curious observation and ends in wisdom, for shards of pottery surviving long-dead and anonymous potters hold a lesson for her: these ancient craftsmen produced not for profit but simply to achieve an ideal blend of utility and design in their vessels. Thea is aware at once of their goal, and by analogy she comprehends the significance of her own voice and the care she must take to attain a comparable perfection. Thus, from a vast historical distance the pre-Columbian potters work a therapeutic effect; and Thea's aims, abraded by life's grinding pace, gradually resume their old validity. Art is eternal, she understands, unalterable through time. When Cather admitted that she had endowed the singer-heroine of *The Song of the Lark* with a good many of her own experiences, incidents such as her discovery of the cliff dwellers were what she meant.[49]

Willa Cather hardly expected the desert to provide her with stimulating companionship, but her discovery of the cliff dwellers coincided with her introduction to a man whose personality so overwhelmed her that for months her letters continued to sing his praises. Julio (Cather gave him no surname) was Mexican, a native of Vera Cruz, and he carried with him to Arizona the somber, experienced mein of an ancient race. His Indian heritage was obvious in his skin, the color of old gold. He could have been Mediterranean except that he displayed neither softness nor sunniness but an indifference and opacity that were magnetic. His eyes brimmed with old trouble, Cather thought, and his long upper lip could have come only from an Aztec sculpture. Cather was intrigued at first, then infatuated. The natural elegance of Julio, something she had never seen before, was certain never to be seen again; there was an eternal quality about him, as if he had no beginning and no end. All in all, Cather felt inadequate to express her feelings except in terms of awe; she mused on methods whereby Julio might be enticed to go East, where she imagined the New York artists competing for his services as a model. Eventually, in June the time came when, no matter how tipsy she might be with the desert and with her Julio, Cather knew that she must leave; she would go bleeding, but she must go.[50]

In the meanwhile, Julio had entertained her with a story of an Aztec queen and her forty lovers, a tale she would have Don Hedger retell in "Coming, Aphrodite!" in 1919. And the night before leaving Winslow, she accompanied Julio to a Mexican ball, an experience reproduced in *The Song of the Lark* when Thea Kronborg accompanies Spanish Johnny to the adobe dance hall in Moonstone's Mexican quarter. Like Cather in Winslow, Thea is the sole Anglo-Saxon in attendance—"one blonde head moving among so many dark ones"—and her response to the dance is the same as Cather's. In contrast to the rowdy railroad-employee dances Thea is familiar with, the Mexican ball is all quietness and softness, and its music is a flow of smooth rhythms. Thea is struck by the dancers' lack of constraint, by their grace and courtesy, their natural harmony of movement, "their greetings, their low conversations, their smiles." The incident marks her farewell to Moonstone, Colorado, just as its prototype marked Cather's farewell to Winslow, Arizona.[51]

In 1915 Willa Cather revisited the Southwest, this time with greater calculation aforehand. Her target now was the Mesa Verde and its recently excavated cliff palace, a 223-room habitation dating from the thirteenth century. With her friend Edith Lewis as a companion, Cather traveled to Denver on the Burlington as it followed the meandering path of the Republican River, the river of her childhood memories, toward its origin; then from Denver they rode the narrow gauge Denver and Rio Grande over the mountains to Durango; and from there, to Mancos, the railroad stop nearest Mesa Verde. In Mancos, still twenty miles from the mesa, Cather located a brother of Richard Wetherill, the cowboy who in 1888 swam the Mancos river on his horse while searching for strayed cattle and found instead the cliff dwellings. In 1915 no automobile road led to Mesa Verde; so the two women hired a team and driver to make the

trip. Mesa Verde had been a national park since 1906, but its isolated position discouraged visitors; thus, because Willa Cather and
Edith Lewis were the only guests for most of a week, the resident
forest ranger, "Jeep," was able to spend most of his time acting as
their guide.[52]

She found it impossible to say anything intelligible about this
glorious country, Cather wrote Elizabeth Sergeant, except that it
drove her crazy with delight. Photographs absolutely failed to do it
justice; it was too large, too grand and various. The ruins that appeared on available postcards were no more than samples, for similar relics were stuck all around the mesa like the nests of birds—
inaccessible, a thousand feet from the closest vantage point. Cather
could examine such ruins with binoculars, but she doubted whether
they could ever be reached. One structure in the vicinity that could
be personally examined, the forest ranger told them, was Tower
House, a yet unexcavated cliff dwelling in Soda Canyon. Since he
could not accompany them, "Jeep" appointed his brother-in-law, a
younger and less experienced man, to be their guide; although they
reached Tower House without difficulty, they became lost in the
dark while returning. Aided on the rough terrain by diggers from an
archaeologist's camp in the adjoining canyon, the women spent most
of the night finding their way back to their camp. It was a very
exacting twenty-four hours, Cather admitted, yet she doubted she
had ever learned so much in any equivalent span of time.[53]

From Mesa Verde Cather and Lewis traveled to New Mexico,
reaching Taos—then an isolated village, not an artist colony—by
wagon over a difficult road. The month they spent lodging in a
primitive adobe hotel there and prowling the countryside on horseback gave them a unique opportunity to study every contour of the
land: its rocks and streams, its flowers and trees, and its human
habitations, chiefly small Mexican villages. Willa Cather was to return to New Mexico time and again in years to come, but already in
this single summer she had soaked up experiences that would stand
her in good stead ten years later when she came to write *The Professor's House;* into this novel the story of the Mesa Verde, disguised
slightly as "Tom Outland's Story," is placed as strategically as a
turquoise set in silver. And Cather's encounter with the New Mexican landscape was to prove equally fruitful, for it would lead directly
to *Death Comes for the Archbishop.*[54]

CHAPTER 3

The Bright Challenge

"Youth . . . makes the new machine,
the new commerce, the new drama, the
new generation; it is Fecundity."
—Willa Cather, 1913

"**Y**OU are older now," wrote Miss Jewett in 1908, when she urged Cather to advance beyond the quality of her early stories. Cather at thirty-five, like the heroine of her story "Ardessa," could no longer claim to be young; and her imperceptible but certain passage into middle age turned what had been a lively concern with youth into an obsession. In her articles and interviews the decisiveness of the early years figured more prominently; in her fiction it became central and remained so for more than a decade. The theme of youthful struggle was related to a backward glance over her own career, for she was now able to see that the years before twenty were the really important period when her own basic story materials had been collected. The articles she wrote for *McClure's* as she phased herself out of that organization are instructive. "Training for the Ballet" (1913), which equates dancers with other artists, explains that a girl expecting a ballet career "ought to begin the first exercise when she is nine years old" and never stop rehearsing until she is ready to end her career.[1] In the lives of dancers, writers, and particularly singers, she found support for her own conviction that there is no substitute for an early start. Geraldine Farrar, the opera star, had studied in Paris when she was fifteen and had made her Berlin debut at nineteen. Olive Fremstad, Cather's favorite, had played the organ before she was ten with wooden clogs tied to her feet in order to reach the pedals. At eighteen Fremstad had arrived by herself in New York, where she sang in churches for three years while she saved enough money to study in Germany where she sang for ten years; and in 1903 when she returned to debut in New York, she had won acclaim. For the young person of talent and dedication, anything was possible. Cather's interviews with Farrar, Louise Homer, and Fremstad, published as "Three American Singers," traced careers to childhood impetus.[2]

A third article reviewed the dramatic season 1912–13,[3] which could be cosidered "a good one" largely because of the staging of Arnold Bennett's *Milestones*, a play that explores the conflict between youth and age. Cather ranged in her analysis far beyond the limits defined by Bennett's drama; in fact, his play conveniently served as a stimulus for her own thoughts: "Youth is the only really valuable thing in the world . . . because it is force, potency, a physiological fact. A kind of power can be extracted from youth that can be obtained nowhere else in the world—or in the stars; and this is the only power that will drive the world ahead."[4]

Youth became the impelling theme of the first substantial efforts of Cather's majority, and she knew no better way to portray its "rocket quality" than to show it in pursuit of the glory of art, a quest she knew intimately. Her fondness for Henry James notwithstanding, Cather had not always considered stories of artists to have valid substance. Shakespeare had shown wisdom, she noted, in not using actors as the heroes of his dramas; and she had not missed the fact that only once had Thackeray written a novel with a novelist at its center. The explanation for caution seemed obvious in 1898: "When you step into a world of productive art you step into a world distorted and your novel is misshapen from its inception because an artist's life, aside from his work, is much like a machinist's shop after the engine he built has gone out; there is nothing but broken tools, the tanks of black water where hot metal has cooled, and gray ashes in the furnace. We want heart rather than temperament in a novel, and the two seldom go together."[5] Ten years later her fascination with esthetic fulfillment had overridden all theory, and she regarded the artist as eminently suitable material.

I *Artists:* Youth and the Bright Medusa

Cather ruthlessly culled her publications for items worth saving as the 1920s opened, and she selected eight stories for preservation: four were resurrected from her *Troll Garden;* four had appeared since 1905. Those from the earlier collection are uniformly stories of success; the others, of failure in its various degrees. Since each story in its own way concerns young Americans and "the madness of art," she titled her book *Youth and the Bright Medusa.* A strange title, but Cather titles have special meanings, sometimes hinted at in epigraphs; or they are perhaps elucidated elsewhere by the author herself. But she made no comment about the title of this new book, perhaps because she thought it self-explanatory—and to an extent it is. The monster Medusa, one of three Gorgons, her head a wreath of serpents, petrified all who dared look upon her with naked eye. To attempt her subjugation lay beyond human power, and most of the countless youths who hunted her to her lair perished. Only the brilliant, redoubtable Perseus was successful, and he approached Medusa obliquely, guided by her reflection in his shield. With her severed head he was enabled to perform great deeds.

On this ancient myth Cather constructs her legends of man's hunt for glory. The analogy with Medusa is imperfect, yet workable, for from Medusa's bleeding torso sprang the horse Pegasus, whose hooves kicked open the fountain of art atop Mount Helicon. Youth and art, the struggle of the one to master the other—she saw this pattern in the legend. Medusa stood, therefore, for life's bright challenge—bright but without mercy—that only the fearless, the able, the resolute might dare approach. The promise that most would fail is no dissuasion because the Medusa of art glitters with the same magnetic appeal as the Medusa of legend. Her attraction is hypnotic and, in the end, ironic. Speaking of the "magical song of youth, so engrossing and so treacherous,"[6] or of "the bright face of danger,"[7] Cather herself leads others to an identification of the bright Medusa as "art itself, with its fascinating and sometimes fatal attraction for youth."[8]

The collected stories interpret the theme variously, but common elements recur. The universals are clear:

Youth: the early years are the decisive ones. Physical vitality is assumed as youth's basic component. The protagonists tend to be middle-aged, and enough of them are fortyish to suggest strong autobiographical involvement with their author. They appraise their youth with the educated eye of hindsight.

Desire: an overpowering motivation must draw the aspirant like a flake of iron toward the electromagnet. Every artist's secret is passion, a will to live and to do, for which no lovely counterfeit suffices.

Ability: without the creative thrust of talent, anticipation of achievement is an empty delusion.

Effort: struggle goes forward with a dedication suggestive of monomania. Any significant diversion of time or attention—no matter how human, humane, or humanitarian—may stop an individual's development and achievement. The aim of all is success, a rare commodity in any shape or form; but authentic success—the perfection of one's talent—is not to be confused with popularity or remuneration. One contents himself with what he has earned; thus the half-loaf is common, and disillusion, endemic. Youth, desire, ability, effort—should any one of these components be lacking or insufficient, failure is foreordained, even potential disaster; the world bears few Perseuses.

The collection opens with a title, "Coming, Aphrodite!" suggestive of a siren's bright lure. Two young artists in the story aim at self-fulfillment. Don Hedger, a painter toiling in the avant-garde has twice declined to produce the same thing over and over, no matter how profitable such "marketable products" might be. He paints in his own manner in the hope that he will give birth to an art the world will recognize and receive as something new under the sun. The other artist is Eden Bower, a singer. Singing at age thirteen for church entertainments, she decides upon her ambition: a musical and acting career, a life spent in great cities, the admiration of many men, and the satisfaction of every material want. These two, thrown together in a rooming house, stand poles apart in concepts of art and ambition. Eden Bower urges her friend to paint the type of pictures that appeal to popular taste. Later, after he has become financially successful, there will be time for him to paint whatever kind of picture pleases him. Eden's visit to the studio of the celebrated commercial painter Burton Ives has awakened in her a craving to afford the same Japanese servants, wine cellars, and riding horses that Ives' "art" supports. When she expresses incredulity at Hedger's refusal to commercialize his painting, he reminds her that the public is most fond of familiar things; and familiarity implies the same thing repeated over and over. He, on the other hand, would rather paint for fellow artists capable of appreciating the rare, individual talent. To Hedger this type of recognition would constitute true success. Eden Bower cannot comprehend such a notion, for her thoughts are on the money to be hers if and when she becomes a really popular singer. "You know very well there's only one kind of success that's real," she informs Hedger.[9]

All of *Youth and the Bright Medusa* hangs on that final sentence, raising the question of success, its meaning and import. But Cather had written: "In the kingdom of art there is no God, but one God, and his service is so exacting that there are few men born of women who are strong enough to take the vows."[10] Don Hedger worships that one God, but Eden Bower kneels to idols. After a momentary blaze of romance, these two go their separate ways; the scene changes to eighteen years later when the aspirants have reached their middle years and have succeeded, each in his own way, for better or worse. Hedger, the more resolute, has forced the world to acclaim his "very modern" canvases. Eden Bower's name blazes in lights above the Lexington Opera House, where she is opening with the Puccini she does so well that she rarely attempts anything else—as she gives the same performance everywhere, the audience can count on its not being different. She has given her public what it wants.

Now that Hedger is forty, his name is on the lips of every young man in the world of painting, he is "decidedly an influence." Eden Bower has acquired a popular following and a face that is "hard and settled, like a plaster cast"; at forty, one wears the face one has earned. Even with the best of fortune, says Cather, "a 'big' career takes its toll." The story combines thematic elements; youthful desire is joined by ability and dedication. The purity of the ingredients determines the quality of the results. As Hedger's dealer explains to Eden Bower, "Madame, there are many kinds of success"; she and Hedger embody two of them.

"The Diamond Mine" defines another price the artist may pay if he responds unduly to the claims people make on him. Cressida Garnet, possessed of unlimited vitality and determination, has risen to musical fame "fighting for her life at first, then for a beginning, for growth, and at last for eminence and perfection." Possessions have held no charm for her, but people have; and she is weighted with family impedimenta—a series of rapacious husbands and a pack of bilious siblings who regard her as a natural resource, a vein of ore, a rich pit in which they may indulge themselves. Cressida, a victim of her own human needs, is forty-two when it dawns on her that her personal relationships always involve dollars.

Cather had written of the artist's time of glory: "If he devotes these years to self-sacrifice, to caring for an aged parent or helping to support his brother's children, God may reward him, but Nature will not forgive him. The kind of self-sacrifice that has so long been accounted a virtue . . . Nature punishes more cruelly than she does any other mistake."[11] And, "At my age," Cressida reflects, "that's a dismal truth to waken up to." Her fortune is wrecked by her fourth husband's speculative forays on Wall Street. Cressida travels to England to raise money through a concert tour, but life has lost its savor: "Why is it? I have never cared about money, except to make people happy with it, and it has been the curse of my life." For her homecoming she schedules a stateroom on the *Titanic*.

"A Gold Slipper" and "Scandal" concern another singer, Kitty Ayrshire, and illuminate an additional peril for the artist. Burning "to try everything," Kitty tries to bridge the distance between herself and her audience. When she crosses the footlights, she is put into disillusioning contact with two of her "fans," one of whom is a Pittsburgh coal king with a contempt for music. Marshall McKann, who follows the crowd to Carnegie Hall in obedience to social ritual, is bored to death and so inattentive that he scarcely bothers to stifle his yawns. Kitty, who has appeared in a daring gown calculated to shock the Philistine crowd in her campaign to "get its money and to make her name a household word," encourages conversation with McKann on the express train back to New York. "There is so much fake about your profession," he tells her. "It's an affectation on both sides. I know a great many of the people who went to hear you tonight, and I know that most of them neither know nor care anything about music." Kitty is driven to defend herself: "If you saw the houses I keep up, and the people I employ, and the motor cars I run—." It is the wrong argument, of course. McKann, with his coal mines, his army of employees, and his vast wealth, is certain to best her.
    In a second incident Kitty allows herself to be the tool of a department-store magnate's vanity. Ostensibly furthering a novice singer's career but actually satisfying her own curiosity, she breaks her rule against private concerts to perform at Siegmund Stein's housewarming. Next morning in the newspapers she finds her photograph paired with Stein's, her name linked romantically with his. When she complains that "People do tell such lies about me," her advisor reminds her "You have enormous publicity value and no discretion." Kitty fancies herself to be at the whim of circumstance, but she is victim of her own urge for novelty—"I wish you would

invent a new Kitty Ayrshire for me," she sighs at one point—and is much too willing to collaborate with her mortal enemy.

Eden Bower, Cressida Garnet, and Kitty Ayrshire lead flawed lives, but the remaining stories in *Youth and the Bright Medusa* recount disasters. "The Sculptor's Funeral" and "A Death in the Desert" concern the simplest and most decisive defeat an artist can meet: death at an early age. Harvey Merrick, an accomplished sculptor with great promise for the future, is dead of tuberculosis at forty. A youthful escape from his depressing Kansas village had been the first step toward glory, but now his coffin is sent by freight to the town he loathed. Those aware of this sad homecoming are Philistine to the core; and judged by their views, Merrick's "failure" could have been prevented if he had only been sent to a first-rate Kansas City business school. Isolated insights come from his apprentice, who escorts the coffin, and from lawyer Jim Laird, who deflates the criticism of the hometowners: "Harvey Merrick wouldn't have given one sunset over your marshes for all you've got put together, and you know it."

"A Death in the Desert" tells of the sudden end of the singing triumph of Katharine Gaylord. In Cheyenne, where she has retreated, ill to death of tuberculosis, her brother states all the facts that are needed: "She had to fight her own way from the first. She got to Chicago, and then to New York, and then to Europe, and got a taste for it all; and now she's dying here like a rat in a hole," in a bitter exile. In her last days Katharine meets Everette Hilgarde, a visiting musician from New York who raises her spirits—if only fleetingly—with rousing memories of former days: the exhilaration of a ferryboat trip from New Jersey, the gleam of the Diana statue atop Madison Square Garden, the happy struggle of music students in the region of Carnegie Hall. "And what do they eat and drink in the world nowadays?" asks Katharine, as she dies unnoticed two thousand miles from the only world she considers real. Her story is one of effort and failure, "the things Keats called hell" and she calls tragedy; but it is scarcely that, if tragedy springs from character. But tragedy or pathos, she suffers deeply from the knowledge that the world rushes on while she perishes. "I lie here," she tells Hilgarde, "listening to the feet of the runners as they pass me—ah, God! the swift feet of the runners!"

While Katharine Gaylord is wrenched unwillingly from her world of art, Aunt Georgiana of "A Wagner Matinée" has renounced it for marriage. The incompatibility of marriage and career is inherent in the situation of the story; they are two worlds, better off unmixed. Although Aunt Georgiana lacked the talent to become a great performing artist, she did have a good future as a teacher of paino, but even this possibility is renounced for a dugout on a Nebraska hillside. The distance between the frontier and the world of Boston musical circles is dramatic. For thirty years in her tall, naked prairie house, Aunt Georgiana knows only a flat world bounded on the east by cornfields stretching to daybreak, on the west by a corral extending to sunset. She is exiled, like Katharine Gaylord, until she scarcely knows that she *is* exiled; all thought of her other life has evaporated in the heat and dust of the Divide. After a visit to Boston, a single afternoon of rapture at a Wagner concert, she realizes what she renounced, what she lost, and *for* what. The news comes like a summons of death; after the orchestra has filed off the stage, she sobs, "I don't want to go, Clark, I don't want to go." Her nephew knows from his own Nebraska boyhood what she means. "For her, just outside the concert hall, lay the black pond with the cattle-tracked bluffs; the tall, unpainted house, with weather-curled boards, naked as a tower; the crook-backed ash seedlings where the dish-cloths hung to dry; the gaunt, moulting turkeys picking up refuse about the kitchen door."[12]

When accomplished performers such as Kitty Ayrshire sing in Pittsburgh, they reside at the Schenley Hotel. Their "fans" like to believe that their idols revel in heavenly luxury, amid flowers and steam heat, with echoes of applause ringing in their ears. Occasionally Cather provides a peek inside the Schenley in order to demonstrate that "success" is not quite what some imagine it to be. Yet the prominent singers possess much of value in comparison to the many who have nothing. "Paul's Case" is the story of one of these, a true loser doomed to stand outside the Schenley in the rain with his eyes riveted to the orange-lighted windows while he dreams of an Aladdin life inside that "tropical world of shiny, glistening surfaces and basking ease."

Even more than Aunt Georgiana, Paul is an object of pity; for his youth can feed only on dreams. Bereft of talent, without even an appreciatory grasp of art, he is altogether unfit to pursue the Medusa. Yet actors and singers fire his imagination, and his belief in fairy stories, in genies rising in clouds of smoke from bottles, fans a burning vision of himself transported overnight from drabness into brilliance. When Paul returns from the Arabian Nights atmosphere of his ushering at Carnegie Hall, his head reels with pleasure; by comparison, his homecoming is a fall from life into death: "The moment he turned into Cordelia Street he felt the waters close above his head. After each of these orgies of living, he experienced all the physical depression which follows a debauch; the loathing of respectable beds, of common food, of a house permeated by kitchen odours; a shuddering repulsion for the flavourless, colourless mass of every-day existence; a morbid desire for cool things and soft lights and fresh flowers."[13]

To obtain these desirables is Paul's sole, morbid thought, for Paul is clearly deranged. He has not the slightest chance of escaping Cordelia Street except through an act of madness, triggered when his father removes him from Carnegie Hall and arranges other employment. Paul steals $2,000 from his employers to finance a "golden" week in New York—the Waldorf, hansom cabs, loge at the opera, champagne, flower-packed rooms, perfumed corridors of an enchanted castle. Then discovery, pursuit; the old feeling recurs that "the orchestra had suddenly stopped, the sinking sensation that the play was over." When all the world is as dark as Cordelia Street, only one escape is possible, and Paul finds his way out: red carnations pinned to his coat, he flings himself beneath the wheels of a locomotive.

Youth, Talent, Desire, Effort—only Don Hedger combines these in a fully satisfactory career. The singers, through haphazard effort or incomplete dedication, come off second best. Poor Aunt Georgiana has lost whatever possibility her youth held; Harvey Merrick and Katharine Gaylord lack life itself; and Paul, with his aberrant desire, is marked from the start for catastrophe.

II *Tamer of Rivers:* Alexander's Bridge

Cather approached the prospect of a novel with diffidence, understanding that a fiction writer in the twentieth century must attempt the book-length tale or be content with a minor career. Short stories alone could never command the audience, hence the reputation, that her ambition required. But writing a novel was something of a sacred venture for Cather, who had written: "It is a solemn and terrible thing to write a novel. I wish there were a tax levied on

every novel published. We would have fewer ones and better."
Moreover, to be a woman was doubly uncomfortable. Although
many women were writing novels, some popular beyond belief, she
felt that the excess of really bad stories they offered placed serious
female writers in jeopardy. She wondered sometimes "why God
ever trusts talent in the hands of women, they usually make such an
infernal mess of it. I think he must do it as a sort of ghastly joke." Yet
Miss Jewett had been a shining exception, and perhaps she would
be also. And, joke or not, the fact was there must be novels.[14]

Understandably, Cather chose to structure her first venture on
the safe formula of the romantic triangle. Bartley Alexander, a famous engineer, faces at middle age a familiar crisis: his professional
success is clouded by an unhappy personal life. His wife, Winifred,
has lost "the energy of youth," and at forty-three he is fearful that his
own drive is going. Groping for some extension of his youth, he
finds it in actress Hilda Burgoyne and decides to leave Winifred for
her, even though the scandal may result in social ostracism. Alexander has a giant project under way, a bridge slung across the St.
Lawrence River in Quebec, and as his personal crisis reaches its
breaking point, so does the crisis in his bridge project. Unforeseen
strains, the result of faulty calculations, cause the bridge to collapse,
carrying Alexander and a number of his workmen to their deaths.

Critics have found *Alexander's Bridge* anomalous. It is dissimilar
to the thrust of Cather's later work, and the author herself considered rejecting it altogether. Later she called it shallow, conventional, and superficial. Regardless of her eventual dissatisfaction with it,
this first novel is built upon the same theme that unifies *Youth and
the Bright Medusa*; for the life of Bartley Alexander much resembles that of Cressida Garnet. The youth of each artisit is told in
retrospect from a point at which the unanticipated burdens of "suc-
cèss" have complicated existence. The novel is full of remembering;
the "impetuousness, the intense excitement, the increasing expec-
tancy" of younger days haunt the characters. Remembered zest
sustains those lost in the "grey" fact of their aging and their inability
to forestall the slide into the "dead calm of middle life." Youth—
the time for dreaming, fighting, accomplishing—assumes definition
as "the energy . . . which must register itself and cut its name before it passes."[15]

Lucius Wilson, Alexander's one-time mentor and a man who has
helped generations take the first precarious steps toward their

Bright Medusa, comments on the way in which some take a bad hurt and lose courage in the race while more fortunate ones clear all hurdles. Bartley Alexander, who "caught the wind early," perseveres for two decades to tame his rivers. Then, at the same age as Cressida Garnet, he finds himself vulnerable when he discovers the price exacted by life. His power has itself become "another kind of restraint"; his life as a bridge builder seems "exactly the kind of life he had determined to escape." Uncertain of himself, he recalls his electric days of youth, and he groans: "That this should happen to *me!*"[16]

Cressida Garnet allows marital and family concerns to whittle away at her, and Alexander suffers from the delusion that his life has room for both dalliance and a career. On the one occasion when he subordinates his bridge building to personal pleasure, disaster results. Because he remains overlong with Hilda, he does not arrive at the river in time to check the excessive strains developing in his suspension span. It falls; he falls.

III   *Faith in the High Land:* O Pioneers!

The decision to center her fiction on the lives of artists required Willa Cather to lay aside her belief that artists were unnatural subject matter. She felt an impelling need to deal with them, but she knew the risk was that she might mine a narrow vein and achieve only monotony. One solution was to reach for variety by treating sculptors, dancers, painters, singers, architects, and writers; and she tried doing so. But this method was more an evasion than a solution, and Cather realized it soon enough.

Immersed in art herself, she tended to confuse esthetics with her true theme, which was not the *artist's* struggle so much as *youth's.* And in her earliest efforts to portray this struggle, failure had predominated. "Peter," "On the Divide," and other stories had told of lives broken by circumstance. So launched, Cather might conceivably have gone the naturalist route had not her intimate knowledge of prominent actors, singers, and writers demonstrated unequivocally to her that conditions are not impenetrable walls too high to scale; they are hurdles that an able individual can clear. There was no need to deny the power of conditions, but merely to emphasize the role played by individual responsibility. The universe was one in which many fell while few rose, just as the naturalists believed; but for Cather the causes were not to be found wholly in the stars. In short, human victory over "life" was possible; and Cather's second first-novel was written from this stance.

O Pioneers! marks a return to the materials of Cather's Nebraska youth, materials that she had refrained from using in recent years, possibly because of the stinging criticism with which stories such as "A Wagner Matinée" had been received at home in Nebraska. She was candid in admitting that these early stories, although absolutely true, were one-sided in their view of the early West and reflected too openly her own impatience at being confined to the isolated plains. Now that she had seen the world and achieved in the metropolis, she felt differently about the fields of home; and particularly with the encouragement she had received from Miss Jewett, she was better prepared mentally to shape her Nebraska experiences into art.[17]

Cather's affection for Nebraska had never dwindled; even more important, the state's influence upon her had not diminished. When she thought it over, her life on the plains seemed to be a long, immense, continued story, one with themes as grand and events as diverse as those in *War and Peace.* The West was a book, one she had begun to "read" as a child; and its plot and characters far surpassed the inventive powers of man. She had read a good deal of this book firsthand, but when absence kept her from doing this, she had friends who would bring her up to date, in detail, on all that she had missed. In this way she was kept abreast of the continuing chapters in the life of Red Cloud and the French and Bohemian country that surrounded it.[18]

Cather seemed to understand instinctively that the land itself must be the hero of her novel, and she told this to her friends Zoë Akins and Elizabeth Sergeant; she explained that she was allowing her story to emerge from the wild land precisely as Anton Dvořák had let the Largo of his *New World* Symphony grow from the long grasses of the plains. She had many apprehensions about such a method; it was a new departure, an untested manner of looking at her materials. While she was writing, she was ready to admit that the novel would either be excellent or dismal; sometimes it seemed to be all crops and cows. All she knew was that the new book was what she had always wanted to write and that she would find it unbearable if she fell down on the job and failed to do justice to her theme. By the time she had completed the novel, however, she was much more encouraged to feel that she had succeeded; and when

Elizabeth Sergeant read it critically and suggested that its structure suffered from lack of a bold skeleton, Cather was ready with a vehement, if good-natured, rejoinder. Miss Sergeant was to remember that the plains country, unlike an area of hilly land with its marked outline of stone and ridge, was composed of soft black soil that ran through one's fingers easily. Cather attributed this quality of plains soil to enrichment by decayed grass rather than the ashes of larger vegetation. She had let it influence the mood of her story, she said, as well as its structure.[19]

Despite its radical difference in locale and method, *O Pioneers!* has more in common with Cather's stories of painters, singers, and architects than might at first be supposed. With a woman as its hero, the novel demonstrates the possibility of triumph over iron-hard frontier conditions. From its first pages Alexandra Bergson is equated with the artists who seek the Bright Medusa because, in Cather's expanding approach to the term, an artist may express himself in any medium. Cressida Garnet sings, Harvey Merrick sculpts, and Don Hedger paints; but for Alexandra, daughter of the Middle Border, "it is in the soil that she expresses herself best."

Alexandra, defined through contrast, is positioned among her family in order to shine more brightly against their weaknesses. The elder of her two older brothers, Oscar, is totally blind to the potential of the Divide (Cather had written that a pioneer should have imagination). Slavish adherence to routine is his crippling vice: "He worked like an insect, always doing the same thing over in the same way, regardless of whether it was best or no," precisely as Eden Bower sings her Puccini over and over as if she were a singing machine programmed to give her audiences what they like. Oscar plods indolently from hour to hour, day to day; he is a mechanism to whom any notion of change or improvement is foreign. At another extreme Lou, the younger brother, is unequipped to establish the simplest economical routine; a leafhopper, he flits in agitation from one inconsequential chore to another while his neglected wheat hangs overripe in the fields. Between these poles stands Alexandra, methodical enough to complete her task, yet free from slavery to repetitious routine; alert to change, she is not erratic but imaginative.

Alexandra is born with the ideal synthesis. Her abilities appear in childhood, just as artistic talent might make itself known in a different Cather heroine. By the time she is fifteen, she knows exactly where she is going; and cloaked in a man's long ulster, she assumes the aspect of a young warrior, a glance of "Amazonian fierceness" on her face. So armed, she is ready upon her father's death to shoulder his challenge, no simple chore. The land is possessed of its own will; it demands "to be let alone, to preserve its own fierce strength, its peculiar savage kind of beauty, its uninterrupted mournfulness . . . like a horse that no one knows how to break to harness."[20] Considering that western roads were only faint tracks in the grass and even the fields were scarcely noticeable, it is understandable that in eleven long years Alexandra's father had been able to make little impression on the land. When he arrived on the Divide, he had passed his hour for doing. Cather had written that the first generation came too late in life: "After a man has passed his fortieth birthday it is not easy for him to change the habits and conditions of his life."[21] But his daughter is young, bent on a mission, infinitely capable, and wholly determined.

Before she is twelve, Alexandra can talk competently of farm affairs and can guess the weight of a hog more accurately than John Bergson himself. Her "strength of will" and "simple, direct way of thinking" serve her well, for a girl farming an untamed prairie needs such attributes. Even so, three hard years of drought pose special problems, she needs the stamina not to retreat to city factories as her neighbors do at the first crop failure. She needs imagination as an artist needs talent—an ability to foresee potential, to recognize her advantages, and to press them.

One additional virtue equips Alexandra to wrestle with the land as Medusa: self-confidence. Faith in one's ability and in the primacy of one's goal has been essential to Cather's singers and painters, and Alexandra declares a similar vow: "Some day the land itself will be worth more than all we can ever raise on it. . . . Down there they have a little certainty, but up with us there is a big chance. We must have faith in the high land."[22] Cather does not pause to document strategy or to anatomize skirmishes, for the novel leaps forward sixteen years. Settlements have rooted, rains are adequate, crops, abundant. As for what the Bergson homestead has become, "Anyone hereabouts would have told you that this was one of the richest farms on the Divide, and that the farmer was a woman."

Were the novel to close on this note, it would be pure and simple escapism; but the spectre of the price that Alexandra pays now enters. Nearly half of *O Pioneers!* is devoted to showing what her achievement costs her. The book has been called "split" by critics who feel that it breaks midway and forgets Alexandra for the tragic romance of Emil Bergson and Marie Shabata; but this split is no more than a shift of emphasis: the thematic center of the story is unimpaired. Rather than being limited to the struggle or its outcome, the attention is turned to aftereffects; and Alexandra remains the unifying figure. Whatever exists, exists for her sake; and this includes the Emil-Marie story, even though its form creates an illusion of separate existence. Even prior to this desolate climax, however, the worm has been despoiling Alexandra's harvest. "We pay a high rent, though we pay differently," she reflects as she considers the rich farm built from her labor: "We grow hard and heavy here. We don't move lightly and easily . . . our minds get stiff. If the world were no wider than my cornfields, if there was not something besides this, I wouldn't feel that it was much worth while to work."[23]

As middle age with its gray cloud of disillusionment darkens her outlook, life appears empty, and Alexandra yearns for satisfactions beyond a career. She searches where Cressida Garnet searched—in her family—and finds what Cather's strong individuals always find—that "no one can build his security upon the nobleness of another person." The price of triumph is isolation, as the singer Olive Fremstad had told Cather, "We are born alone, we make our way alone, we die alone,"[24] a thought that Cather felt to be true. For a true artist, no escape from the knowledge of loneliness exists.

Alexandra reaches for contentment with Carl Linstrum, but she finds his weakness incompatible with her own power. Their "romance" has been sporadic; it promises never to be wholly satisfying, merely a piece of salvage from wreckage. Then the old disparity between Alexandra and her brothers grows. They refuse to acknowledge their sister's skill; as time goes on, they delude themselves into thinking that theirs was the true faith, that they built the Bergson empire. Inevitably a break occurs, and Alexandra's lament is that of every Cather artist: "I wonder why I have been permitted to prosper, if it is only to take my friends away from me."

On Emil, the baby of the family, Alexandra pins her fondest hopes, fashioning him as her surrogate. In that world wider than her cornfields, he will have "a chance, a whole chance." His function, in her eyes, is to provide the full meaning of her long struggle. But her hope, grounded upon an illusory child-parent relationship, is doomed. Emil drifts into his impetuous love intrigue with Marie, and both are shot to death by Marie's husband beneath Alexandra's white mulberry tree. One finally cannot squeeze more from life than life is prepared to yield.

IV   A Condition of Spirit: The Song of the Lark

The definitive study of the artist is *The Song of the Lark*, about which revolve a dozen shorter sketches either preparatory to the major work or spun off from its momentum. Derived from hundreds of reviews of artistic performances; from innumerable contacts with actors, singers, writers, painters; and from forty years' immersion in the artistic struggle, this novel of all Cather's books—and quite fittingly—proved the most interesting to write. The working title under which it was begun in 1913 tells why, for *Artist's Youth* compresses into two words the concern then spilling over into every project she undertook.

Alexandra only dreamed of a world wider than her cornfields, but Thea Kronborg ventures forth to subdue it. Her career synthesizes those elements of artistic struggle that the stories in *Youth and the Bright Medusa* dramatize piecemeal. Thea is born with all the requisites; and even the subculture of Moonstone, Colorado, recognizes the extraordinary quality of her voice, a potential apprehended anew by each of her singing coaches. Her perennial beau, Fred Ottenburg, summarizes the phenomenon: "It all goes back to her original endowment, her tremendous musical talent." What of the drive essential to shaping this raw talent into a perfect medium? "There is only one big thing—desire," says Herr Wunsch, Thea's first music teacher; he is confident that Thea has the "rocket quality" youth needs: "she will run a long way; they cannot stop her!"

Hard work is no obstacle, for Thea quite fully understands what will be demanded. She meets difficulties with "imagination and a stubborn will," for her fierce self-assertion points her always toward that single final goal: "A great many trains . . . carried young people who meant to have things. But difference was that *she was going to get them!* . . . As long as she lived that ecstasy was going to be hers. She would live for it, work for it, die for it; but she was going to have it, time after time, height after height."[25] The rewards arrive, as they did for Alexandra.

In fact, an abstract of one novel would approximate that of the other. In both a capable aspirant devotes her youth to a diligent struggle for achievement; success won, her attention turns to mitigating the isolation of fame with satisfactions in the personal sphere. Yet the novels, so similar in theme, are worlds apart in the telling, particularly in matters of proportion. The struggle of Alexandra is a blank page bridging sixteen years of work and planning, but in *The Song of the Lark* the struggle itself dominates the novel with a detailed account of Thea's climb, ledge by ledge, up the musical peaks to her Everest, the Metropolitan Opera House.

Because the heavily documented novel was, by and large, not something Cather admired, her method in *The Song of the Lark* seems aberrant. A partial explanation for the direction taken may be found in "Plays of Real Life," her portmanteau review of the 1912–13 Broadway season. In Edward Shelton's *The High Road*, the pertinent drama, the heroine, Mary Page, the pampered mistress of wealthy Alan Wilson, tires of idleness and decides to become a personality in her own right, even if it requires her to begin in a shirtwaist factory at $6 a week. Her arrival at this decision closes act 2; act 3 occurs years later, with Mary Page president of the Women's Industrial League and author of a shelf of labor-movement tomes. Perseverance has carried her to the top; she marries the governor of New York and assists him in a campaign for the national presidency. So far so good.

Cather spends a good deal of time and space on *The High Road*, not because it is fine or bad, but because she has a point to establish. Shelton's leap in time between acts 2 and 3 is disturbing, for no audience could genuinely understand a woman's emotional and spiritual revolt merely by hearing her argue her case, "even though she argues well." Mary Page has done something remarkable, true: "But the eighteen years in which she accomplished this, in which she struggled and suffered and grew stronger, and began to help other struggling women, are a closed book to us. . . . The growth of the girl who left Wilson's flat, that night, into a woman who works for other women, would be an interesting development to follow; and such a character, made real and living, would be fresh dramatic material. But Mr. Sheldon omits her struggle, everything that made her what she was, and asks us to take the really dramatic part of her life for granted."[26] Determined not to sin by the same omission, Cather adopted the method—though not the outlook, surely—of the literary naturalist and wrought a minutely detailed presentation of surfaces.

Her decision—at times it seems her obsession—not to omit any-

thing of the record may follow from the fact that there is much of
Cather herself in the novel. Few writers better understood the
effort required to perfect an art; few felt more directly the renuncia-
tions imposed by a major career. If one removes from the novel the
singer and the song, substituting in their places the writer and the
story, the result approximates the saga of Willa Cather. She was
unwilling, of course, to offer her publisher an autobiography in
fictional dress, as a literary naturalist might perhaps have done
without undue blushing (but even the chief of them, Theodore
Dreiser, altered his hero's occupation in The "Genius" from writer
to painter as he approached a final draft).

Among the prima donnas of her day, Cather came upon a singer
whose career roughly paralleled her own. Her years as a critic made
music a natural choice, yet she needed a life around which a multitude of details might cluster. She found this in the story of Olive
Fremstad, then at the height of her popularity at the Metropolitan
Opera. In 1913, when Cather interviewed Fremstad, Louise
Homer, and Geraldine Farrar and offered their careers as examples
of significant American achievement, any of the trio might conceivably have served as a model for her heroine. But the life of
Swedish-born Olive Fremstad—who "came out of a new, crude
country, fought her way against every kind of obstacle, and con-
quered by sheer power of will and character"—bore an uncanny
resemblance to Cather's own experience. Just a year older than
Cather herself, Fremstad had immigrated with her parents at the
age of six. Her childhood was spent in St. Peter, Minnesota, a
village (not unlike Red Cloud) no more than an unpromising crossroads "where there was neither artistic stimulus nor discriminating
taste." To step from St. Peter to the stage of the Metropolitan Opera
required special attributes; and Fremstad, in Cather's eyes, "wrung
from fortune the one profit which adversity sometimes leaves with
strong natures—the power to conquer."[27]

Upon meeting, Cather and Fremstad struck up an instant friendship grounded on the middle-western upbringing they shared. Not
everyone could be expected to comprehend what tied them to each
other, for their relationship was like that of the two accomplished
New Yorkers who meet on the train in My Ántonia and agree "that
no one who had not grown up in a little prairie town could know
anything about it. It was a kind of freemasonry." Cather appears to
have recognized at once that Fremstad must be the model for the

singer in her new novel. Her overwhelming impression was one of awe, of being struck dumb in this presence; it was as if she had discovered on the pavement of New York one of her strong women from the Nebraska Divide, a battered Swedish mother with the diffident, courageous, and farsighted eyes of a pioneer. On Good Friday, 1913, after hearing Fremstad perform the role of Kundry in *Parsifal*, Cather watched the singer as she stepped into her carriage, her eyes empty and glasslike after giving every ounce of her energy to her performance; Cather wanted to shout *hurrah!* in the street. Invited to Fremstad's apartment, she was even more certain that this phenomenon belonged on the Divide, for her furnishings, which created the incongruous impression of a forest of gold legs intermixed with heavy Mission-style oak, were precisely as Cather had envisioned the home of Alexandra Bergson to be in its prosperous years.[28]

Willa Cather turned to her novel very soon after having met Fremstad, and in four happy weeks late in 1913 was able to finish twenty-eight thousand words of manuscript. Her enthusiasm over the marvelous Fremstad increased as she worked; she felt herself to be an explorer who had discovered not a new country (those seemed relatively easy to find) but something rarer, a new kind of human being. During the following June Cather visited Fremstad at her summer home in Maine. The house required three fires, and Fremstad chopped the wood for all of them. In addition, the singer tended the gardens, did the cooking, tramped the hills, and fished as if it were up to her to provide subsistence. Everything was done strenuously up in Maine, even the nighttime dreaming. Altogether, Cather was impressed by the most magnificent display of graceful human vitality she had ever witnessed, it struck her, imaginatively, as something like living with the wife of the dying gladiator in the depths of a German woods.[29]

Because music was a field she loved but had not studied technically, Cather employed professional help when her manuscript was completed to assure that embarrassing errors did not occur. She was delighted at her music critic's enthusiasm for the story and relieved that he found few points needing correction. With justifiable pride she could report that her aide was able to predict from reading early portions of the novel precisely what qualities Thea's voice would possess in her later career. To be this successful was gratifying, for the novel was a difficult one to write, and to have come through without a catastrophe was enough to make a novelist pant with relief. When the book appeared late in 1915, Fremstad and Cather met coincidentally in Lincoln. Now on tour, Fremstad had purchased a copy of the novel at Brentano's before leaving New York. Cather was apprehensive that her heroine might not care for some parts of the story; in particular, she was fearful that she might have spoiled the book by making Thea's professional triumph too conventional, the type of success that was meaningful to Thea's hometown neighbors but perhaps superficial to an artist. To hear Fremstad, in person, express high and unreserved praise for her accomplishment was as much as Cather could ask for.[30]

The Song of the Lark focuses upon art, and the principles extolled in the novel are those that were treasured by Cather herself and reinforced and given a new articulation by Fremstad. They include the notion that not only is one's art the single thing worth sacrificing for but that the perfection of art is worth any sacrifice one must make. Of all life's beauties, Fremstad told her, "art is the only thing that *remains* beautiful." Cather had found that dedication mandates loneliness; and Fremstad confirmed that an artist's isolation arrives as a direct consequence of his choice. "The artist's quest is pursued alone," she told Cather; "the highest rewards are, for the most part, enjoyed alone."[31] To Cather, cheap compromises had the seeds of death in them; and Fremstad believed one must aspire to nothing lower than absolute perfection.

Fremstad in all ways seemed an unflawed artist in contrast to Geraldine Farrar, who had confessed in her interview that her talent was limited. There existed "frozen heights" of music inaccessible to her. She could not climb them; she did not hunger to reach them; she was content. But at least one singer, Cather discovered, was "now aspiring to and attaining those frozen heights of which Miss Farrar speaks"—Fremstad. She embodied the American possibility, and she brought truth to Theodore Roosevelt's definition of Americanism as "not a condition of birth, but a condition of spirit." Goethe, Cather recalled, had spoken of many kinds of garlands. Some were easily gathered on a morning's walk, but the only garlands worth having were the unattainable. Never gathered, never to be gathered, these represented a final frontier for the human spirit; and pursuit of them was "one of the most glorious forms of human activity." Fremstad seemed the only kind of artist worth the effort of a major novel, and while *The Song of the Lark* is no biography manqué, its outlines and some incidents are suggested by Fremstad's career.[32]

The principle of contrast established in *O Pioneers!* is continued in *The Song of the Lark* in order to define the superiority of Thea Kronborg's accomplishment. She is encircled by partial and total failures against whose deficiencies she glows. Conditions, influential as they may be, need not be decisive: "Everybody's up against it for himself, succeeds or fails—himself." Talent, youth, health, passion, and dedication are major determinants; and each of the failures has fallen short in one respect or another. None but Thea possesses every essential. Thea's Aunt Tillie as a girl "couldn't help believing that she would some day have to do with the 'wonderful'." Untalented Aunt Tillie exists on dreams that mark her as an eccentric; for she can achieve only vicariously. While performing in Kansas City, Thea treats her to a week's visit and allows her the run of her dressing room, where she rummages through trunks of theatrical costumes, wigs, and jewels, like a child. Aunt Tillie is a subject for compassion, like Paul or Aunt Georgiana; but Thea has only scorn for the thin talent that falls prey to flattery—and such meager but overblown talents abound. Lilly Fisher, soloist with the Moonstone Baptist choir, has a trick of combining songs of sentimental appeal with declamatory pieces and is much in demand locally; but having tested the limits of her ability, she comes to naught. While studying in Chicago, Thea observes Jessie Darcey, whose concert voice betrays "every quality a singer ought not to have"; she "sang off pitch and didn't mind it." Beneath her bravado Jessie is terrified, as bewildered by her popularity as Thea. Jessie and Lilly instruct Thea in the dangers of confusing the popular with the fine.

To say there are many kinds of success is to speak of varieties of failure. Herr Wunsch, Thea's childhood coach who suffered a loss of nerve, comes to mind when Lucius Wilson, in *Alexander's Bridge*, speaks of talents crippled by early hurts. When Thea takes piano students of her own, she is disappointed in the brightest of the lot, Jenny Smiley, whose fine pianist's hands and quickness in reading music are limited by a lack of desire. She doesn't "care a rap" for a career, Thea observes; "she has no pride." Thea's Chicago coach, Madison Bowers, had once been a baritone of promise but he never makes a big career, although singers with less native equipment have become prominent names. Bowers lacks warmth and enthusiasm; his "long, sallow, discontented face" betrays him. A cold

contempt for his audiences that they can feel prevents him from
developing fully, and he ends his life teaching singing and piano to
the wives of millionaire brewers. By Chicago standards Mrs.
Katharine Priest is a top-rated singer, but her supreme self-satis-
faction holds her back from higher aspirations. She is a person, Thea
believes, who should not be allowed to exist in happy ignorance.

Katharine Priest may have been invented to illustrate Geraldine
Farrer's reluctance to attempt the heights; but a second Farrar
observation—that one's voice is an instrument to be "played upon
intelligently, not knocked to pieces"—is illustrated in another singer, Madame Mecker. Mecker is a true artist, a great one, the only
immortal Thea has met in New York; but to reach the frozen heights
she has paid a terrible price. A "bad method" adopted in her impatience to reach the top has produced instant results but wrecked her
voice. "She's breaking up too early," Thea discovers, "just when she
ought to be at her best." Mecker's is the saddest failure of all, but
her single mistake is one more than nature forgives.

"The failures are swept back into the pile and forgotten," Thea is
told; "they don't leave any lasting scar in the world, and they don't
affect the future." Because her own aim at perfection is never
deflected, Thea manages to identify and avoid every temptation,
while the disasters around her comment ruefully on the pitted and
boulder-strewn obstacle course an artist must travel alone. Yet the
solitary way is the only sure way. Cather had written admiringly of
Fremstad that no other singer had "managed to live in such retire-
ment," an island of self in the city's flood; "work is the only thing
that interests her."[33]

The novel flies like a banner its triumphant key sentence: "O
eagle of eagles! Endeavor, achievement, desire, glorious striving of
human art!" But for all of Thea's fidelity and for all her triumphs, her
personal affairs wither as her career flourishes. To her friend Dr.
Archie after her operatic stardom is assured, Thea laments the
jealousies and disappointments she cannot avoid. "You get to hating
people who do contemptible work and still get on just as well as you
do. There are many disappointments in my profession, and bitter,
bitter contempts." Once again life demands its price; "anything good
is—expensive."

In an epilogue that hobbles somewhat infirmly upon the striding
heels of the major action, twenty years have passed; and the name of
Thea Kronborg is synonymous with musical greatness. Knowledge

of the psychic costs of her career have prompted her to look belatedly for happiness somewhere other than on a stage before an applauding audience, and she marries Fred Ottenburg; but marriage for her is no more a panacea than Alexandra Bergson's union with Carl Linstrum. Both are afterthoughts, attempts to beat the bargain made with life. These late marriages might be interpreted as concessions to a "happy ending" formula, but this explains them less than to see in them Cather's own resistance to life's apparent refusal to allow one both a career and a family. The marriages arrive less as triumphs for her heroines than as consolation prizes.

V   *Rich Mine of Life:* My Ántonia

Superficially the story of Antonia Shimerda seems cut from a quite different piece of cloth than its predecessors. A Bohemian girl, she is trapped in the worst possible conditions on the Nebraska Divide: indentured to a town family, uneducated, bereft of special talents, so trusting as to be easy prey to a glib scoundrel. Yet, maintaining a steellike equanimity, she becomes a farmer's wife, mother to a houseful of happy children. Hers is the rarest of Cather's lives—a joyous one.

For Ántonia, no iron bridges span obedient rivers, no spread of prairie transforms into pasture and cornfield, and no audiences pay homage to a perfect aria. The professional career underlying previous stories is entirely removed, allowing Cather to show "just the other side of the rug, the pattern that is supposed not to count in a story."[34] Celebration of professional fulfillment broadens to a struggle for personal identity. Ántonia's instinct plunges her always into life's mainstream, disregarding money, position, possessions, or career. To live merely for the rich experience of living itself is the "career" she labors at with as much diligence as Kronborg ever practiced her scales. One thinks of Thoreau withdrawing to Walden purposely to confront life, drive it into a corner, and derive its essential quality—all to determine whether it be mean or fine and finally to be able to say that he had lived. So armed with a fierce necessity to breath and act, Ántonia rises relatively unscathed from ordeals that might ruin a lesser spirit. Lacking any "talent," she possesses the gift of a warm heart, a buoyant sense of humor, and an infinite capacity for enthusiasm.

This pursuit of life—not to achieve any lofty aim but merely to go with the tides, to exist fully, passionately—was foreign to Cather's nature. But the more she came to understand the toll exacted by a career, the more attractive seemed the life given over wholly to immediate experiences, and the more she came to admire—almost to envy—those equipped to approach their lives in this seemingly easy fashion. Cather could never truly comprehend such persons, the Ántonias of the world. The Thea Kronborgs, the Alexandra Bergsons she knew intimately, for they were so nearly surrogates for herself. In contrast, Ántonia Shimerda required not analysis but worship. She was to be marveled at, something like a Sequoia that stands forever in contradiction of all one's experience.

Thus Cather needed to contemplate her heroine from a safe distance in order to protect herself (as author) from an involvement so intimate that it might reveal her inability to project the girl's personality firsthand. When Cather was writing *The Song of the Lark,* her delight at and fascination with the creative process had allowed her to crawl temporarily inside the skin of another individual. But this was not possible with Ántonia; she and the Bohemian girl had too little in common.[35] Cather's solution was to tell the story through the viewpoint of a relatively detached narrator. It was a relatively common device, much used by Henry James, that Cather's knowledge of painters and their methods would seem to have suggested. Elizabeth Sergeant remembers a discussion of artistic form and technique that occurred in the spring of 1916, when Willa Cather was beginning *My Ántonia.* Cather learned forward suddenly, took a Sicilian apothecary jar filled with orange-brown flowers, and placed it alone on an antique table. For a moment she might have been a painter setting up a still-life arrangement. "I want my new heroine to be like this," she said, "like a rare object in the middle of a table, which one may examine from all sides. I want her to stand out—like this—because she *is* the story."[36]

The narrator whom Cather selected, Jim Burden, allows for Ántonia to be examined in this manner and the various "sides" from which she is seen correspond to the different ages at which Jim knows (of) her—as a child, as an adolescent, as a maiden in full bloom, and finally as a mature woman. Because Jim Burden himself grows older as the story progresses and because his experiences alter him as Ántonia's experiences alter her, each successive view or "side" from which she is observed is more complex and more interesting. At the same time, the adoption of Jim's point-of-view not only explains but actually mandates the episodic structure of the novel. In the introductory chapter Jim is shown as he emphasizes the personal nature of his memoir: "He . . . wrote on the pinkish face of the portfolio the word, 'Ántonia.' He frowned at this a moment, then prefixed another word, making it 'My Ántonia.' That seemed to satisfy him."[37] The most effective way for Jim to create the really strong impressions that will make the manuscript-Ántonia *his* and not another's is to see or hear of her at widely scattered but fairly regular intervals—above all at moments of significance in her life. This, of course, is the manner in which the novel proceeds.

Even though Sarah Orne Jewett had warned Cather about the risks involved in using a masculine viewpoint in fiction, Cather felt that in this case nothing but a male narrator would suffice, hazardous as the experiment might be and artificial as it might appear if she failed. Her decision to use Jim Burden was not happenstance but, on the contrary, carefully reasoned out. Ántonia was to be created from a group of real-life models, and since the most interesting things about these women had been told to Cather by men, she felt that logically Ántonia's story should be presented through the memory of a man. Because the novel was to be a story of feeling, rather than a flurry of plot and action, Jim Burden would tell it in the first person; thus would the emotions involved be best expressed. To establish the nostalgic mood that would color the novel, Cather borrowed from Russian and French literature the device by which an author (unnamed, but clearly Cather herself) meets the narrator (Jim Burden) on a transcontinental train: the pair reminisce about a person (the Bohemian girl) they both knew as children, an experience that triggers the narrator's written account—the remainder of the book.[38]

Cather's introduction was calculated to serve a further purpose: that of establishing about Jim Burden certain important facts that affect the story he tells. A mature man of the world, he is able now to evaluate Ántonia's worth more fully than he could at an earlier, less experienced age. Because he is childless and unhappy in his marriage, he tends to look backward rather than forward; therefore, his dwelling with such concentration and sympathy upon his early, happy years—and the Bohemian girl who influenced them—is made more plausible. Finally, Cather felt that the struggle she had gone through in order to ghostwrite S. S. McClure's autobiography, and the resounding success she had made of it, had equipped her to handle a masculine viewpoint convincingly. She felt she had been able to "become" Mr. McClure because she knew him so thoroughly; she was positive that in *My Ántonia* she could achieve the same success with Jim Burden because (although she declined to name a specific individual) she intended to base her narrator on a man she knew fully as well as she knew McClure.[39]

In its elementals Ántonia's story tallies with the novels preceding it: a young person's struggle, obstacles to be surmounted, contrasts sharpening the central actor's achievement. But, the world of art aside, Ántonia surpasses previous Cather protagonists in maintaining an integrated personality. It is for her to avoid Thea's dry preoccupation, Alexandra's sense of confinement, and Bartley Alexander's dread that middle age will be a dark cloud blotting the sun from his universe. One need not search outside the novel for comparisons, however, for a contrast with the conventional success story is built into the fabric of *My Ántonia* itself. Jim Burden, in his forties, is a member of an important New York legal firm, is instrumental in the progress of a great railway, and is married to a handsome woman of social prominence. But the reader knows him to be far from fulfilled; his childlessness and marital estrangement dampen his spirits, and his greatest thrill seems to derive from opportunities to sponsor others' dreams, now that his own are over. By contrast, Ántonia in her middle years shines "in the full vigour of her personality, battered but not diminished." She is at the close of the novel fully as life loving as she was when, an immigrant girl of fourteen and bright as a new dollar, she rode the Burlington into the Nebraska plains.

Her secret is enthusiasm—to retain a child's delight in existence. Her effervescence contrasts with the aridity of lives around her. The tone is set when in the opening pages of the novel, Jim Burden thinks of Ántonia and her difference from his "unimpressionable" wife, so "temperamentally incapable of enthusiasm." Set down on the raw Divide, where Ántonia's great desire to learn alerts her to every aspect of the wild land, she contrasts with her own depressive father, who is Cather's last fictional rendering of the Sadilek suicide that never loosed its grip on her imagination. In Black Hawk, town girls are but pale tintypes beside the living, breathing vigor of the immigrant girls, of whom Ántonia is the prime representative. Eventually, those daughters of merchants and tradesmen—trapped in their mystique of "refinement," corseted literally and figuratively by the demands of convention and reared with blind trust in their natural superiority—provide too simple a contrast; and the phenomenon of Ántonia must be presented within her own small circle. For she is not wholly typical; Tiny Soderball, to cite one instance, who becomes the greatest worldly success among the immigrant group, dwindles into "a thin, hard-faced woman, very well dressed, very reserved in manner. . . . like someone in whom the faculty of becoming interested is worn out."[40] Ántonia is cut from sturdier goods; she wears well, showing her quality even when threadbare.

In her struggle to tame life, Ántonia gropes; fumbling repeatedly, she runs a zigzag path but makes relentless progress. If ever there were a true-born victim of circumstance, it should be she: a stranger, unacclimated to frontier life, unable to speak the lingua franca, socially outcast, with a defeated dreamer for a father, a harridan for a mother, a sullen lout for a brother. But Ántonia transcends every disadvantage and does so without soiling herself. Every day she runs barefoot to the Burden home to pick up a few English phrases. No corner of the plains is exempt from her inquiring eye. She is no scholar, of course, for there is no time for school: "I ain't got time to learn," she tells Jim; "I can work like mans now. My mother can't say no more how Ambrosch do all and nobody to help him. I can work as much as him. School is all right for little boys. I help make this land one good farm."[41]

Lacking the resources of an Alexandra, she cannot erect a farming empire; instead, yielding to inevitable conditions, she goes to town as hired girl to the Harlings, where she is exposed to new ways and put in touch for the first time with civilized refinements. She throws herself into those aspects of social life open to Bohemian girls, but she keeps her individuality intact by refusing to drop the new friends made in the "dancing school" tent, even when refusal to conform threatens to cost her the household post on which she exists. When at last Ántonia is betrayed in the only way she could be, self-blinded to the hypocrisy of the railroader who seduces her, this betrayal and the child she bears leave her self-esteem unscarred. Eventually, with the man meant to be the "instrument of her special mission," she mothers her large family, giving herself without reservation to the renewal of life. Those close to Ántonia see her life as ideal. To Cather she is cause for celebration; she justifies the human race.

To what extent the story of Ántonia Shimerda fits into the characteristic pattern of "artist's youth" is a question answered by Cather herself, and in the simplest manner. Of the painter, writer,

sculptor, singer there is no question; but in the new dimension
Cather includes as artists "the German housewife who sets before
her family on Thanksgiving Day a perfectly roasted goose" and "the
farmer who goes out in the morning to harness his team, and pauses
to admire the sunrise."[42] Ántonia's function is to epitomize this
group: "One of the people who interested me most as a child was the
Bohemian hired girl of one of our neighbors, who was so good to me.
She was one of the truest artists I ever knew in the keenness and
sensitiveness of her enjoyment, in her love of people and in her
willingness to take pains."[43] After celebrating the ultimate professional achievement—a portrait of success exceeding Thea Kronborg's is inconceivable—Cather caps her theme of youthful struggle
with the saga of this hired girl's personal triumph. The entire story is
a paean, and no Cather heroine evokes such admiration as this
Bohemian girl who is so warmly eulogized as the novel ends:

She lent herself to immemorial human attitudes which we recognize by
instinct as universal and true. . . . She was a battered woman now, not a lively
girl; but she still had that something which fires the imagination, could still
stop one's breath for a moment by a look or gesture that somehow revealed the
meaning in common things. She had only to stand in the orchard, to put her
hand on a little crab tree and look up at the apples, to make you feel the
goodness of planting and tending and harvesting at last. All the strong things of
her heart came out in her body, that had been so tireless in serving generous
emotions.
It was no wonder that her sons stood tall and straight. She was a rich mine of
life, like the founders of early races.[44]

CHAPTER 4

The Reign of Mammon

"I have always felt very much as though
I were keeping the Ear Gate of the
town of Mansoul."
—Willa Cather, 1902

B Y 1920 Willa Cather had published in rapid enough succession
four novels defining the "rocket quality" of youth pursuing the
Bright Medusa and was ready to collect the cream of her short
stories reinforcing that major theme. Unless she were to repeat
herself—a prospect she found abhorrent the idea had nowhere
further to go. Every significant aspect had been dramatized, and the
definitive triumphs in art and in life had been achieved in *The Song
of the Lark* and in *My Ántonia*. Yet themes rarely loose their grip on
a writer overnight, and Cather's works of the 1920s and the 1930s
continue to display strong traces of her early preoccupation.

One of Ours (1922) is torn between two themes. The theme
woven around the momentum of the artist's youth carries onward,
but Cather's principal concern has altered to center upon the larger
struggle engaging civilization with barbarism. Claude Wheeler, a
young man of uncertain abilities, has a blazing desire for accomplishment, but he has no passionate reason for being: "the old
belief flashed up in him with an intense kind of hope, an intense
kind of pain—the conviction that there was something splendid
about life, if he could but find it!"[1] With this sentence a gulf opens
between Claude and the young artists who are guided almost genet-
ically toward their pole stars; for from their early teens they know,
like Cather herself, precisely where they are going.

Following *One of Ours*, the theme of young struggle dwindles. In
A Lost Lady (1923) and in *My Mortal Enemy* (1926), the aspirant is
removed from the center and relegated to the frame of the picture,
reduced to a narrator's position. Young Niel Herbert's efforts to

become an architect are so overshadowed by the narrative of Marian Forrester that his personal struggle is no more than hinted at; chiefly, the reader sees him catching his train for college or arriving home on summer holiday. And one knows that Nellie Birdseye, the narrator in *My Mortal Enemy*, is involved in an identity crisis, but her career aspirations are never told. One hears her exclaim, "I know what I want to do, and I'll work my way out yet," and that is all.

Godfrey St. Peter of *The Professor's House* (1925) is an academic analogue for the Cather artists who pause in maturity to take stock. Familiar traits identify him, such as his conviction that, "if there were an instrument by which to measure desire, one could foretell achievement." St. Peter has persevered in solitude, writing his books in his own way regardless of their immediate reception. He has maintained as much faith in his own high land as Alexandra maintained in hers. Much like Don Hedger, who paints for the future and is finally vindicated, St. Peter lives to hear his name on the lips of all whose concern with history is genuine. But this quick sketch is soon over. In the process of moving from his old house to his new, St. Peter is forced to confront the society that has grown up around him while he has worked alone; and Cather writes about this society. St. Peter's development as an artist merely serves to provide her with a handy route to her new interest.

Death Comes for the Archbishop (1927) is the archetype of youth's struggle subordinated to larger affairs. The triumph of strong young dedication over conditions serves as the narrative backbone; but Father Latour has formally renounced personal ambition, and any "success" he achieves must necessarily be interpreted in terms of the broader society he serves. Only once in Cather's later work does youthful aspiration form the center for a novel. *Lucy Gayheart*, something of an anachronism in 1936, properly belongs with *O Pioneers!* and *The Song of the Lark* (it derives, in fact, from a 1911 story of "the gayest—oh, the gayest!" girl in Riverbend, Nebraska). Lucy is a rather bloodless cousin to Thea Kronborg; for, possessed of a small talent, she hopes for a career but will not wrestle for one with an unwilling world.

Having finished with concentration upon youth, Willa Cather turned her eyes in another, but related, direction. The use of literature as a tool of social protest held no charm for her; when only twenty-one, she had written that whatever the novelist's mission might be, it surely was "not to clean the Augean stables." One drawn to such an aim would do better to join the Salvation Army.[2] A conviction so deeply felt must have endured considerable strain at the offices of the muckraking *McClure's*. But a rigorous criticism of life is implicit in Cather's writing from its beginnings—a muted impulse to expose, to satirize, to reform. Her pause for a hard look at the social landscape in which her strong individuals sought their identities and rewards gave Cather good reason for dismay. Observing the directions America seemed to be taking, she was pessimistic in the extreme; for order appeared ready to break into chaos. Idealism suffered painfully at the hands of a pervasive expediency, art degenerated under the impact of commercialism, and the nation seemed bent on abandoning its soul in a scramble for the dollar—and what culture had been preserved was threatening to disintegrate.

Cather had written that for an artist two ways were open: toward the true and the beautiful, or toward the clever and the comfortable. These alternatives held true also for the nation, and America's drift seemed a hazardous one. As she saw it, the country had turned its back upon spiritual ideals and was falling to its knees in idolatry of the material. After 1918 this present danger became the thematic center for her novels.

I   *Skirmishes in a Holy War, 1895–1920*

Cather's concern with societal values appears in her first published story, "Peter," in which an opening dialogue pits art against dollars. The aging musician resists his son's demand that he sell his violin. "I need money," argues Antone; "what good is that old fiddle to thee?" The instrument's worth, "enough to buy a new hay rake," measures the distance between father and son. In another early story, "El Dorado: A Kansas Recessional" (1902), men flock to the West not to build or civilize but to exploit for profit. Theirs is a dog-eat-dog society, and each man is so intent upon "his own particular dream of fortune" that the whole pack is easily swindled by blackguards so preposterously cunning that they go unsuspected. Fleeced, the entrepreneurs pack up and leave the new buildings of El Dorado to deteriorate. In this story Cather initiated a view of frontier life that never failed to dismay her; and in the 1920s the spectacle of her "geliebtest" land at the mercy of moneygrubbers became her major lament.

When Willa Cather encountered Pittsburgh in 1896, the face of that city foretold America's future: a forest of skyscrapers rising on limited available land space, sooty smoke belching from industrial chimneys, open-pit furnaces turning the night sky rosy. Here was true exploitation of both men and resources, and acquisitive pursuits lorded it over culture. Cather preferred to see the culture, but she did not close her eyes altogether to what was evolving on the banks of the Monongahela. In 1902 her story "The Professor's Commencement" indicted Pittsburgh. Its central figure, Professor Emerson Graves, had come to Pittsburgh intending a temporary stay, but he remained to oppose the complete despoiling of the area.

An early-day ecologist, Graves is among Cather's first recruits in the warfare between ideal and material, and he first defines the struggle: " 'This city controls a vast manufacturing region given over to sordid and materialistic ideals. Any work that has been done here for aesthetics cannot be lost. I suppose we shall win in the end, but the reign of Mammon has been long and oppressive. You remember when I was a boy working in the fields how we used to read Bunyan's "Holy War" at night? Well, I have always felt very much as though I were keeping the Ear Gate of the town of Mansoul, and I know not whether the Captains who succeed me be trusty or no.' "[3] Rather than flee to refuge, Graves stays to "cry the name of beauty so loud that the roar of the mills could not drown it." For thirty years he keeps the gate for culture, and uncertain at the end of his life as to whether his fight is won, he calls upon the coming generation to sustain the struggle. "The Professor's Commencement" is important as Willa Cather's first overt step toward the second of her major themes. Emerson Graves is the first of the "trusty Captains" who hold the Ear Gate of Mansoul.

"The Willing Muse" (1907) suggests the nature of strife between a commercially successful hack-writer and a dedicated artist. The one grinds out stories on a conveyor-belt schedule; the other is adamant in writing only what he must, regardless of time, payment, or critical acceptance. The story's obvious relationship to the Medusa theme is heightened by the fact that the two writers are married; but in joining the larger issue between the esthetic and the commercial, Cather takes tentative steps toward Thea Kronborg's credo: "If you love the good thing vitally, enough to give up for it all that one must give up, then you must hate the cheap thing just as hard. I tell you, there is such a thing as creative hate!" And such creative hate sours the marriage in "The Willing Muse." When Kenneth Gray, husband of the hack-writer, visits his home town of Olympia, Ohio, he finds it "ruined completely. Capital and enterprise have broken in even here. They've all sorts of new industries, and the place is black with smoke and thick with noise from sunrise to sunset"⁴—Pittsburgh again, in miniature. At this point the story transcends its concern with personal ambition, and Cather's two themes grip hands.

In 1909 *Harper's Magazine* published "The Enchanted Bluff," a pivotal story in Cather's emerging concern for the life of the spirit. The story is in two parts. In the first a group of boys lounge by their campfire on the banks of a western river dreaming of a legendary mesa beyond the horizon, a "big red rock" emblematic of the youthful urge to seek, to explore, to find. Unanimously, the boys resolve to seek out the heights. In the second part, after a projection forward in years, the reader learns that of all the resolute young men, not one has managed to hold to his course. Each has been seduced by life's paraphernalia, and most have relinquished entirely their ambition to reach the mesa. Noting of one, now a Kansas City stockbroker, that he "will go nowhere that his red touring car cannot go," Cather speaks of all. In "The Enchanted Bluff" her major themes again intertwine. The aspirants have allowed themselves to be dissuaded from the difficult trek; the pressures of a thing- and dollar-oriented society have bound their souls to the plain.⁵

The destructive impact of materialism on frontier hardiness is first explored in depth in the novelette "The Bohemian Girl." Even as a boy, Nils Ericson, son of a Swedish pioneer, senses that the wholesome dedication of his father's generation is giving way to greed. After leaving Nebraska and traveling widely, he returns to find mondacity riding high, the free life on the Divide stifled, and his own family thinking of nothing but its vast tracts of farmlands. His brothers, interested only in making money, are hostile for fear Nils may have returned to claim his inheritance. The Nebraska wealth means little to Nils, but he is angered by its effects on Clara Vavrika, once his childhood sweetheart and now married to his brother. Recalling Clara's delight in life, he is shocked to find her embittered and works to persuade her that elopement with him is her only hope. "This is a perfect ferret fight here," he argues; "you live by biting and being bitten. Can't you remember what life used to be like?" The only viable answer to a society bent upon stamping individuals into standardized patterns, Cather suggests here, is flight. Indeed, "The Bohemian Girl" is her first story built upon the escape motif.[6]

In her stories of the 1910 era, Cather's disenchantment with the direction taken by society recurs, typically in muted tones, as in "Behind the Singer Tower" (1912). Hallett, the construction engineer of a new skyscraper hotel in New York, rides a ferryboat across the Hudson and from its deck contemplates the mass of stone and steel that characterizes modern America. The forest of incandescent billboards huckstering beers, corsets, and perfumes seems suddenly repulsive; and he wonders whether this kind of thing cannot be overdone: "A single name could be blazed too far. Our whole scheme of life and progress and profit was perpendicular. We depend upon the ever-growing possibilities of girders and rivets as Holland depends on her dikes."[7] Hallett voices Cather's repudiation of the national emphasis upon a brick and steel façade that acts as a cosmetic to disguise illness of the spirit.

New York City serves also for "Consequences" (1915), in which young heirs—a lost tribe that F. Scott Fitzgerald would soon make popular—gorge themselves on the material feast in the metropolis, that "brutal struggle of men and cars and machines"; finally, their wealth squandered, they end as suicides. The story's single strong figure is a woman who, miraculously to all concerned, has "retained something, just enough of the large Western manner. She had the habit . . . of using all our ingenious mechanical contrivances lightly and easily, without over-rating them." At her home the sad young men absorb from her enough "zest for life" to achieve—but only momentarily—"safety—absolute sanctuary—from everything sordid and petty." Once again flight to refuge is suggested as an answer.[8]

But no sanctuary exists for Paul Wanning of "Her Boss" (1919). Wealthy, but on the verge of death, his eyes are opened to the pernicious "desire to possess material objects, to buy what other people were buying" that has infected all America. Paul's house is full, much too full, of things; it is crammed with adult toys. But Paul himself, "the human creature who gathered and shaped and hoarded and foolishly loved these things, he had no chance, absolutely none." Like Everyman, he discovers only on his deathbed the truth of his vanities.[9]

As a group, these early stories point the way toward Cather's

concern with modern values, and at times—"Consequences" and
"Her Boss" being cases in point—the emerging theme already assumes an emphatic position. Still, when collecting her stories in
1921, Cather included none of these; she was engrossed in shaping
her summary statement of the artist's struggle. Inevitably, however,
the broader concern runs in a strong undercurrent through *Youth
and the Bright Medusa*. Since neglect of a rigorous career effort
constitutes a major hazard for artists, one theme complements the
other. The heavy hand of materialism intrudes on artistic life only to
blight, as the collected stories suggest. "Coming, Aphrodite!" contrasts steadfastness with artistic susceptibility to "shabby compromises." The gulf separating the worlds of Don Hedger and Eden
Bower is signified by their irreconcilable reactions to the lavish and
luxurious studio of Burton Ives, society painter. Hedger sees it as "a
very good department-store conception of a studio," while Bower
finds it "gorgeous" because it supports her notion of success, one
measured by the things money can buy, the "one kind of success
that's real." Later, when Bower feels "an utter fool" for having jilted
Hedger, it is principally because the prices of his paintings have
risen beyond limits. There is a reason why Cather has given Bower
the hard, settled countenance she wears as she leaves the gallery
where this news has come to her.

"The Diamond Mine," "A Gold Slipper," and "Scandal"—as their
titles suggest—speak of the sorrows that secular standards inflict
upon those attempting service to the temple of art. The persons
close to Cressida Garnet in "The Diamond Mine" covet only her
money; their rapacity feeds like mold on her rich talent. One after
another her husbands raid her store to satisfy their vanities, and the
only ungreedy one, Bouchalka, is seduced into indolence. Her wast-
rel son cares that she pay his gambling debts, nothing more; but the
most irritating thorns in her side are her brothers and sisters. Envy
sends them ravening after the "material evidences" of her achievement; and they sponge on Cressida's productivity, pervert her desperate need for friendship, and exploit her sense of familial responsibility.

When Cressida dies, their parasitism surfaces nakedly: "The Gar-
nets quarreled over her personal effects. They went from floor to
floor of the Tenth Street house. The will provided that Cressida's
jewels and furs and gowns were to go to her sisters. Georgie and
Julia wrangled over them down to the last moleskin. They were

deeply disappointed that some of the muffs and stoles, which they remembered as very large, proved when exhumed from storage and exhibited beside furs of a modern cut, to be ridiculously scant. A year ago the sisters were still reasoning with each other about pearls and opals and emeralds."[10]

In "A Gold Slipper," Kitty Ayrshire, despite her urge to become "a thoroughly paying proposition," is still a fine artist. Her regrettable flaw is her vulgar need to mingle with thing-oriented persons who can do her harm. Her conversation on the New York-Pittsburgh express with coal magnate Marshall McKann exposes the polarity of their two lives and their disparity of goals. McKann is among Cather's most fully presented portraits of the Philistine: "Heaven knew he never went to concerts. . . . as if he were a 'highbrow' from Sewickley, or some unfortunate with a musical wife. . . . A man went to concerts when he was courting, while he was a junior partner. When he became a person of substance, he stopped that sort of nonsense."[11] Nevertheless, under the press of social amenities, he finds himself at Kitty's concert and, bored to death, endures it to the end. He is a man hostile to all enthusiasm, to individualism per se, to any change except one that might promise him more efficient coal-mining machinery or transport him with greater speed to the far-flung points of his commercial empire. He is congenitally hostile to art and to artists, a most hazardous individual for Kitty to be experimenting with. She feels she can, with impunity; but in both "A Gold Slipper" and "Scandal," she is burned by the fire she plays with.

The Kansas Philistines in "The Sculptor's Funeral" stare at the palm leaf atop Harvey Merrick's coffin without the foggiest notion of what it might signify. In their universal regret for the tragedy of Harvey's life—synonymous to them with the money the sculptor's father "wasted" on his son's education that he might better have poured into Sand Creek for all the practical good it did—the citizens are opposed only by lawyer Jim Laird. "You wanted me to be a shrewd lawyer," he explodes at them. "Our veteran here wanted me to get him an increase of pension, because he had dyspepsia; Phelps wanted a new county survey that would put widow Wilson's little bottom farm inside his south line"—and so it goes round the circle of "mourners." Young men with strength of character are lacking because their elders "drummed nothing but money and knavery into their ears from the time they wore knickerbockers." The story releases a blast of indignation that Cather must have harbored for some time.[12]

In "Paul's Case" life's baggage is confused with the real thing. Sight of "a satin gown and a tiara" throws Paul's world out of focus. On his holiday stolen to realize his dreams in one final orgy, Paul wonders "that there were honest men in the world at all. This was what the world was fighting for, he reflected; this was what all the struggle was about . . . he knew now, more than ever, that money was everything."[13] Sunk past all coherence, Paul is spokesman for an entire lost generation; and this larger implication gives his case a significance beyond pathos.

II   *Trusty Captains: The Early Novels*

Willa Cather's novels from 1912 through 1918, preoccupied with the definition of youthful struggle, sketch the rising tension between ideal and material. The climax of *Alexander's Bridge* stems inexorably from the architect's first compromise with cheapness. Alexander understands that his Moorlock span is the least satisfactory job he has undertaken—even before it falls—because, in order to end a disagreement with the project's financiers, he has allowed money to speak louder than principle. He finds himself "cramped in every way to a niggardly commission . . . using lighter structural material than he thought proper." The sponsors have insisted on cutting corners, and Alexander's agreement to use an untested procedure is made against his better judgment; he knows it to be expedient and extremely hazardous. Nevertheless, he has given in to pocketbook pressures. As the giant bridge takes shape, he confides to his assistant that he was never justified in assuming that what was safe for an ordinary bridge would serve for this much longer span. At the first warnings that all may not be well, he laments his failure to quit the job when first pushed, but it is too late. Sarah Orne Jewett's caution that Cather must know the cheap thing for what it is and never make believe about it is put to immediate use in this first novel. Repentant too late, Alexander has been a sleepy sentry in the holy war.

Corruption of second-generation Nebraskans is probed in *O Pioneers!* The novel sets Alexandra's Amazonian figure against a society corrupt in its tastes and petty in its dealings. The sons of the pioneers inhabit a world altogether diminished, and the source of the difficulty is expressed in Alexandra's reflection that the land "woke up out of its sleep and stretched itself, and it was so big, so rich, that we suddenly found we were rich, just from sitting still." New wealth eats like acid through frontier ideals, spreading discontent. As mania for standardization drives uniqueness from the Divide, the wealth of the pioneer linguistic heritage is obliterated; Lou Bergson prides himself on speaking "like anybody from Iowa," and his wife develops a terror of being "caught" speaking Swedish at home. The new feeling invades the houses, where living rooms copy commercial display windows and dining rooms must be stuffed with highly varnished chairs, colored glass, and fussy china sufficient "to satisfy the standards of the new prosperity." Corruption is not limited to the cornfields, and one function of Carl Linstrum, newly returned from the city, is to touch on the general failure to maintain quality. What he has seen—the profusion of cheap metalwork, the touching up of miserable photographs, and the vulgarization of good drawings—has sickened him.

The menace works pernicious results among the families. On the threshold of personal happiness, Alexandra hears her suitor branded a fortune hunter; and her brothers forbid her to place "our property, our homestead" in a stranger's hands. They have forgotten that when times were hard they had advocated selling out and retreating to the factories; and they have also ignored their sister's long-standing determination to create the biggest, best-run, and most profitable farm in the region. The dissension among the second-generation Bergsons is one of the saddest pages Cather ever wrote, for the idealistic vision of old John Bergson shatters forever when Alexandra is obliged to dismiss her greedy brothers: "Go to town and ask your lawyers what you can do to restrain me from disposing of my property. And I advise you to do what they tell you; for the authority you can exert by law is the only influence you will ever have over me again." Personal relationships are in tatters; communication reduced to legal memoranda is the ultimate dehumanization. "I think I would rather not have lived to find out what I have to-day," says Alexandra.[14]

The Song of the Lark traces the rise of Thea Kronborg as a singer, but the heroine swims upstream against a materialistic current. Thea, who proves a dependable soldier, is eulogized by Cather as a fighter for ideals, one who is continually at grips with people whom "she had always recognized as her natural enemies." Those who sell out earn Thea's creative hate; and once the battle-lines are drawn, she affords them "no creature kindness, no tolerant good will." The flood of money promised those willing to forsake a higher development has little effect on Thea, but on all sides the fallen tempt her to join them. Madison Bowers, the talented coach, is responsible for her first major disillusionment when he shows himself quite willing to help a "lame" singer establish a popular career if her husband's checkbook warrants it. He reaps a "golden harvest" coaching lumbermen's daughters and brewers' wives and, because of his influential position, is particularly culpable. To his rationalization that a singer's public pays her way and that she therefore must provide what is liked, Thea replies with an outburst: "Well, that's the money I'll have to go without." Her reward for fighting the good fight is suggested when citizens of her home town consider the two young people who have put Moonstone on the map. One is a boy who went to Omaha and built a great fortune; the other is Thea Kronborg. "They do, however, speak oftener of Thea. A voice has even a wider appeal than a fortune."[15]

In *My Ántonia* the spectre of materialism haunts the town of Black Hawk; against its baleful effects a resolute Ántonia stands out dramatically. Cather continues her unsympathetic portrayal of western small-town people who, chained to their prosperity, are misshaped by possession. All things seem to work together to produce rubber-stamp standardization. Black Hawk gives little leeway to culture, even less to breadth of mind. Commerce is fast becoming life's chief concern; individuality is banned. Black Hawk girls, prisoners of a rigid respect for convention, can expect lives spent perpetuating the social status determined by their fathers' positions and property. A Black Hawk boy will fare little better, for he will spend his life in service to "a brand-new house with best chairs that must not be sat upon, and hand-painted china that must not be used."

In this circumscribed world those robust creatures from the Divide, the hired girls, are looked at askance. They menace the established order, roil the proprieties. Ántonia, untyrannized by "respect for respectability," is free to maintain her eccentricities, if only she will. She and her friends have not yet lost their strong, independent natures, their power of honest response, their hearty, invigorating joviality. Their freedom shocks Black Hawk, but they succeed precisely because they are not yet intimidated. They are content to be "different." They accept any available work, making no social distinction between herding cattle and sewing for a merchant's wife.

False modesty has passed them over. Town boys may cast wishful glances at the girls but are too controlled to break caste; and as time passes, the girls typically are claimed by young men from the Divide. They prosper, and eventually Black Hawk merchants find themselves competing to peddle machinery to rich farms presided over by their one-time scullery maids.

Individualism is not all that simple or successful, of course, because Ántonia's charmed circle itself is not impervious. There is, for one, Tiny Soderball, who travels to the Klondike to run a small hotel and eventually owns prosperous mining claims. But the enterprising Tiny succumbs to avarice, the beginning of all misfortune. In 1908 the narrator of the novel comes across "a thin, hard-faced woman" who frankly admits that nothing interests her but making money. This is Tiny, once the gayest of Ántonia's friends, and her story is one of a series of separate panels whose effect is to illuminate Ántonia's triumph. The tale of Wick Cutter and his wife is another. Cutter, a moneylender who amasses a considerable furtune by the squeeze, the hard-nosed deal, and the outright cheat, is a keeper of the flame in the temple of Mammon. He hates his wife so thoroughly that to prevent her from inheriting, he shoots her through the head. Then, for additional assurance, before he turns his gun on himself, he hails passing neighbors to witness that his life extended beyond hers. For the Wick Cutters, money pulls the strings—and people dance.

III *Paradise Lost:* One of Ours

My Ántonia was issued as a disillusioning war drew toward its end, and it was four years before Willa Cather published another novel. When *One of Ours* appeared, her emphasis upon personal destinies was clearly in the process of being superseded by a broader theme. The old world of struggle and idealism had fallen to a new society loving money too much and so dominated by the machine that it let itself be reconstructed as one. Faith in the power of individual achievement had tumbled before the onslaught of standardized man. As a result, a sense of irretrievable loss, one bordering on despair, pervades "Nebraska: The End of the First Cycle," the retrospective essay that Cather published in 1923. Beginning as a paean to those who built the West upon a bedrock of indomitable character, the essay ends as an elegy for a world lost. In it Cather announces that "the splendid story of the pioneers is finished." Although she continued to look to the Middle West as the last best hope of a generation to "challenge the pale proprieties, the insincere, conventional optimism of our art and thought," she was compelled to recognize that her beloved West was stamped with "an ugly crest of materialism." Its manifestations could not be ignored:

Too much prosperity, too many moving-picture shows, too much gaudy fiction have colored the taste and manners of so many of these Nebraskans of the future. There, as elsewhere, one finds the frenzy to be showy: farmer boys who wish to be spenders before they are earners, girls who try to look like heroines of the cinema screen. . . . The generation now in the driver's seat hates to make anything, wants to live and die in an automobile, scudding past those acres where the old men used to follow the long corn-rows up and down. They want to buy everything ready-made: clothes, food, education, music, pleasure.[16]

Money and the machine, the delusion that to live easily is to live happily—these seemed the major threats to her West—and her nation. Cather's dim hope that the new generation might have inherited integrity sufficient to reject this "heaped up, machine-made" existence was expressed only in the most guarded of tones, for the first cycle on the frontier had come to an abrupt halt, and its successor was to be dreaded.

The elegiac tone of Cather's "First Cycle" essay is also the tone of *One of Ours*, which opens upon Nebraskans enslaved by the riches their wild land has produced. Where a man might once have been said to own his land, the land now determines his coming, his going, and his spending. Becoming richer, the farmer sacrifices individuality to humdrum homogeneity. The New carries the field with "a kind of callousness" that Cather finds repugnant. Nebraskans now "destroy the old things they used to take pride in." Fine old cottonwood groves, so ideally suited to the plains, fall to the axe; orchards die of neglect; farmers furnish their houses with ill-made carpets and draperies; and they clothe their bodies in awkward if fashionable apparel. Societal harmony is jarred as property disputes turn neighbors into enemies. Cather could recall pioneer fathers settling their differences amicably; but their sons—stingy, grasping, extravagant, lazy—feel more at home in courtrooms.

One of Ours is Cather's pivotal novel in which her theme of personal heroism gives way to the hitherto subordinated concern for an endangered society. From 1922 her central contemporary figures possess little grandeur, and where the heroic is possible, it occurs in the historical past and never again in the present. Her twentieth-century protagonists tend to be victimized by a misguided society or to collaborate fatally with it. Claude Wheeler is typical; an anonymous recruit in a mass army, he is deluded and destroyed.

In the farm home on Lovely Creek, life is changing. Mrs. Wheeler, old Mahailey, and Claude cling to what they can of an idealism that is only a memory. Mr. Wheeler and the other sons, Bayliss and Ralph, embrace new pragmatic ways. The struggle within the Wheeler family is the struggle within the nation. Mr. Wheeler is callous and unthinking; for example, when his wife mentions she has no ladder tall enough to let her pick her cherries, he chops down the tree, his notion of a fine joke. Serious concerns are limited to plans for more land and larger crops, sharp dealing with the neighbors, and speculation about how high war might drive the price of a bushel of wheat.

Bayliss Wheeler operates an implement store in Hanover, drives a new Cadillac, and believes, as his guiding maxim, that everything has its price. His brother Ralph, who remains on the farm, succumbs in the grand manner to the national mania for machinery: "When the farm implements and the automobiles did not give him enough to do, he went to town and bought machines for the house. As soon as Mahailey got used to a washing-machine or a churn, Ralph, to keep up with the bristling march of invention, brought home a still newer one. The mechanical dishwasher she had never been able to use, and patent flat-irons and oil stoves drove her wild."[17] The passion for new things that money will buy is accompanied by a distorted value placed upon cash itself. Ralph's father quite happily peels off a roll of bills to pay for a new thresher or car, but he thinks it the height of extravagance to buy a meal at the local hotel dining room. When Claude meets his friend Ernest Havel in Hanover, he cannot treat him to dinner for fear of raising eyebrows in a community whose standards tally with his father's; the friends share a home-packed lunch on the creek bank.

Claude Wheeler—his initials perhaps not accidentally those of Willa Cather transposed—represents Cather's sad bewilderment at a society that tells a man to consider himself odd if he tries to think through a problem and explain himself logically, if he dresses with care and taste, or if he is caught taking pains in any concern. Claude is a loser, from the first page of the novel. Spruced up to attend the circus in Hanover, he is ordered to transport a messy load of stinking hides into town because just then the price is good. Claude is eager to attend the State University, but he is sent instead to Temple College, a small denominational school that costs less. But, more important, his father trusts its mediocrity to keep Claude "less likely to become too knowing, and to be offensively intelligent at home." Claude comes to understand this attitude, but he sees no solution. His forced return to Temple buttresses his conviction "that the things and people he most disliked were the ones that were to shape his destiny."

The grotesquerie that passes for life on Lovely Creek is epitomized by a scene wherein Mr. Wheeler, having bargained for a new ranch in Colorado, allows Ralph, who is to act as its proprietor, to loot the homestead systematically of whatever makes life fine and comfortable. Before his apathetic mother's eyes, Ralph raids her fruit cellar for its preserves and jellies. In Hanover he goes on a spree, buying up things, things, things—whatever might make life easy or diverting: guns, saddles, bridles, boots, coats, phonographs, a grand piano, a billiard table. From Claude, who is to remain at home and therefore will not need it, he takes the dress suit his brother had used at the university. No one opposes Ralph's plunder except Mahailey, the old servant woman, who scores a surreptitious victory by secreting the best of the feather beds and hiding the most desirable peach preserves in an old cook stove that, not being new, is safe from Ralph's grasp.

Relatively ineffectual, although close to perceiving the sharp divisions being drawn in the holy war, Claude questions "the use of working for money, when money brought nothing one wanted." His brief stay at the university, achieved at considerable expense to his relationship with his father, has opened his eyes to a life in which cash and machinery might play a proper role. In Lincoln he frequents the home of a cultured family, the Erlichs, who, though poor, live a rich life: "They merely knew how to live . . . and spent their money on themselves, instead of on machines to do the work and machines to entertain people. Machines, Claude decided, could not make pleasure, whatever else they could do. They could not make agreeable people, either. In so far as he could see, the latter were made by judicious indulgence in almost everything he had been taught to shun."[18] But those things in which the Erlichs indulge themselves judiciously—music, books, intelligent conversation, manners, art, "all things which might make the world beautiful"—are Claude's too briefly. He is removed from the university and drawn back into the stifling environment on Lovely Creek.

Claude is victimized finally by World War I, which he sees in a golden haze as a great crusade; and that it might prove counterfeit is inconceivable to him. One day he comes upon his mother reading from *Paradise Lost;* her reciting aloud a passage she finds admirable impels mother and son into a conversation centered on the need to defy wickedness actively. Even in the Bible, Claude reminds his mother, "the people who were merely free from blame didn't amount to much." She replies, "You are trying to get me back to Faith and Works," and of course he is. Faith is not enough, hope is not enough, and blind reliance upon Providence is not enough—these Claude knows; but he sees no way of effectively taking arms against the things he despises. As a student of history, however, his interest centers on Joan of Arc, whose single-handed activism in defiance of overwhelming odds seems "miraculous" to him. When war comes, his eargerness to enlist is linked emotionally with the saint's holy war and with the land in which she waged it, France.

"I never knew," Claude reflects shortly before his death by German machine-gun fire, "there was anything worth living for till this war came on. Before that the world seemed like a business proposition":

No battlefield or shattered country he had seen was as ugly as this world would be if men like his brother Bayliss controlled it altogether. Until the war broke out, he had supposed they did control it; his boyhood had been clouded and enervated by that belief. . . . but the event had shown that there were a great many people left who cared about something else. . . . He knew the future of the world was safe; the careful planners would never be able to put it into a strait-jacket—cunning and prudence would never have it to themselves.[19]

Claude dies with his illusion intact. But because he serves as a medium for Cather's own bitterness and it survives him into a devastating backlash of postwar disillusionment, the futility of his sacrifice must be demonstrated. Claude's mother is shocked at society's alacrity in returning to the meanness and greed that the war had merely interrupted. She gives thanks that Claude died in France because she knows that Claude had to die in order to be saved; he could not have survived the psychic shock of "that last, desolating disappointment"; On this dark note the novel closes. That *One of Ours* is an angry and bitter novel owes less to the influence of the wasted death of Cather's soldier-cousin, upon whom it was based, than to the author's implicit acknowledgment that the holy war for America's soul had foundered.

IV Anchorless: A Lost Lady

Marian Forrester, heroine of *A Lost Lady*, may be regarded as a victim of America's materialistic thrust; but she is first of all its collaborator. The environment in which this fine novelette proceeds is all-important because Mrs. Forrester—lacking dynamics of her own and relying instead upon beauty, charm, and sexual attraction—usefully reflects the people and things of her era. In that period when the original frontier generation yields to the second and lesser one, society is in upheaval. Sunset falls on the pioneers, the new day dawns on a crasser world; Marian Forrester is cut adrift, truly lost, between these two worlds.

Her story rides the surface of massive societal struggle, but Mrs. Forrester is not an active participant on the side of the angels or their opposites. Rather, she represents the spoils of war—a natural dependent who becomes the trophy of the winner. One encounters her as a lovely young woman sheltered by her husband, a retired railroad builder, who provides her money, extravagant apparel, and a ranking position in frontier society that she enhances with her own gay vitality. Captain Forrester, an ideal of the doer, is the first and last of the great constructive personalities; handsome, capable, cultured, he is wealthy through his own efforts, and he possesses great integrity. He is virtually a pillar of the West; and together, he and his wife are unassailable in their heyday.

Awaiting his chance is Ivy Peters; symbol of the corrupted generation trailing downward from the noon of the homesteaders, he is ugly, crafty, uncouth, grasping, and devoid of any sense of fair play. Forrester and Peters embody the tensions between old society and new. By their deeds one knows them: Ivy Peters slits the eyes of a woodpecker and looses it into a darkened world; Forrester sacrifices his personal fortune in order to save small depositors in a wrecked bank linked with his name.

The question of the Forrester marshlands affords Cather a chance to make a central issue of the West concrete. The Captain had built his home in a small valley—half pasture, half marsh—a spot selected for its natural beauty. Ivy Peters covets it, for drained, it promises to yield profitable crops of wheat. In Ivy's eyes this land is one of those "profitable bits" of the West that Cather saw butchered by the new exploitative breed. When Ivy at last does attain financial superiority over the Forresters and the marsh comes into his hands, the despoiling of these lovely but nonproductive acres is an occasion for Cather to make her theme explicit:

The Old West had been settled by dreamers, great-hearted adventurers who were unpractical to the point of magnificence; a courteous brotherhood, strong in attack, but weak in defense, who could conquer but not hold. Now all the vast territory they had won was to be at the mercy of men like Ivy Peters, who had never dared anything, never risked anything. . . . All the way from the Missouri to the mountains this generation of shrewd young men, trained to petty economics by hard times, would do exactly what Ivy had done when he drained the Forrester marsh.[20]

The ruination of the marsh, which is centrally positioned in the book, represents the obliteration of the beautiful by an insensitive and grossly utilitarian society. Mrs. Forrester herself, as the most beautiful object in the novel, is also despoiled by the crass men who covet and eventually possess her.

Marian Forrester may be regarded as a hothouse flower who flourishes under ideal environmental conditions. The wealth, position, protective care, and parade of admirers resulting from her marriage to the Captain furnish her with a solarium existence in which she sparkles. Her laugh, "a soft, musical laugh which rose and descended like a suave scale," reminding one of dance music heard through doors that open and shut, is her most delightful attribute. And she is always laughing—and being given occasion to laugh—within the environment to which her laugh is the natural and appropriate response. One of those Cather characters perfectly attuned to their settings, she is, however, fragile and dependent: "Life was so short that it meant nothing at all unless it were continually reinforced by something that endured; unless the shadows of individual existence came and went against a background that held together."[21] Like the spring flower that flourishes on cool, damp days but fades when the summer sun broils the land, Marian Forrester faces a crisis when her background does not endure. Her husband suffers physical disability and then financial failure; then come hard times, the decline of the railroad, the Captain's continued infirmity, and eventually his death. Without the Captain she is "like a ship without ballast, driven hither and thither by every wind."

Niel Herbert, the narrator of the novel, believes it would have been better for Mrs. Forrester to have perished with the era that nurtured her. Instead, she prefers life on any terms; but she survives as a dry husk of what she had been, a tawdry and somewhat shopworn souvenir. Her beauty fades rapidly, her disposition coarsens, she takes to the solace of alcohol, and she is obsessed with the idea of money. The Captain had been a solid buffer between her and the world of Ivy Peters; now, alone, she had small defense against his aggressive moves. Because Ivy is clever about money, she allows him to invest her small savings, closing her mind to the knowledge that he uses it to swindle Indians of their land. Soon he is admitted to her embrace, then to her bed. In search of a protector, she has found a predator; and when she urges Niel to "hurry and become a successful man," her image of success has clearly become a worldly one. Her admonition—"Money is a very important thing. Realize that in the beginning; face it, and don't be ridiculous in the end, like so many of us"—certifies her fall.[22]

To be sure, there is a final rescue for Marian Forrester, who following her degradation meets and marries a wealthy South American. Once again, with a kindly protector and a climate of wealth, clothes, and admirers, she flourishes. A good deal of her former charm seeps back, as a neglected plant provided with water turns green again. But to Niel Herbert she is lost irretrievably. The Captain had built a bulwark against greed and vulgarity, and she had failed in its defense.

Niel exists chiefly to represent the author and her attitude. Cather drafted the novel in the first person, later altering it; and she herself explained that Niel is not a character at all but "only a point of view," a "peephole" into the world of the Forresters, "something for Marian Forrester's charm to work on." Cather's beautiful memory of the central figure was the thing—the only thing—Willa Cather hoped to accomplish with *A Lost Lady*—just "a delicate face laughing at you out of a miniature," no more.[23] But she does much more; for, though the novel stems from the memory of a lovely lady, it grows also from the confrontation between two worlds: one old, honest, generous, and eminently habitable; another new, false, grasping, and ugly to view.

Marian Forrester herself is an emblem for the Old West—in Cather's eyes, she is beautiful and desirable; but, helpless in deciding her own destiny, she is reliant entirely upon the good will of those who take possession. The West, which had been blazoned far and wide as the "Garden of the World," required generous gardeners; and so it is with Marian Forrester. Possessed by the great of soul, she prospered; when the narrow succeeded, she suffered. "An artist has an emotion," Cather explained, "and the first thing he wants to do with it is to find some form to put it in, a design. . . . It may tease him for years until he gets the right form for the emotion."[24] The ghosts in a writer's mind were nagging always for bodies, she said; and her lost lady—along with her "geliebtest land," the West—found embodiment in this parable of a glorious past degraded by a lesser present.

V   Dead and Gone Indians: The Professor's House

Granville Hicks once complained that Willa Cather did not attempt to see the realities of contemporary life, by which he probably meant that she would not allow her books to serve the same purpose of social protest that he had espoused in the 1930s.[25] Yet The Professor's House in 1925 had taken a hard look from two viewpoints at the contemporary world. The first, a method Cather had used previously, was to see it through the eyes of a man of high dedication, who is dismayed at what lies about him. The second, marking the beginning of an important trend, was to see current society against the backdrop of an older and often better world. In The Professor's House that more desirable world was inhabited by the ancient cliff dwellers of Colorado. Cather's 1915 visit to Mesa Verde bore fruit now in the form of "Tom Outland's Story," a seventy-page interpolation for which Cather consciously broke open her otherwise chronological narrative in order that Outland's account of an ancient Indian tribe might not only contrast with, but actually revitalize, the stuffy atmosphere dominating the modern portion of her novel.

The gray world into which Outland's story brings light is that of Godfrey St. Peter, professor and historian. St. Peter stands at a crossroads in life; and his alternatives are represented by his two houses, one old, the other new. In the house of his past, he has shaped a monumental work on the Spanish adventurers in America; in it, he has known security, its walled-in garden being "the comfort of his life"; and his barren third-floor study, much like that provided

Cather at McClungs', is a retreat in which he might pursue scholarship without distraction. His new house, erected with prize money awarded the first volumes of his history, is comfortable, grand, and showy; but St. Peter cannot avoid feeling uneasy about it. He has managed until now to resist the crass spirit that seems to pervade the world, but the ostentation of his new house seems a major concession. He feels guilt and impotence.

If Claude Wheeler's family was ranged against itself in the holy war, St. Peter's is split even more bitterly; for the forces of Mammon are strong. Her husband's sudden fame and affluence provide socially ambitious Mrs. St. Peter with an opportunity to shed her former life as ruthlessly as the farmers on Lovely Creek consigned theirs to the rubbish heap. Novelties captivate her—new clothes, new furnishings, new mechanisms, new friends—and the prize surmounting all is her lavish house, newly completed and waiting for occupancy; but St. Peter resists the move. The family is divided also on the issue of a revolutionary vacuum tube invented by the Professor's protégé, Tom Outland. Killed in World War I, Outland willed his discovery to St. Peter's daughter Rosamond, and the invention is being exploited with considerable profit. But the money is destructive; it shatters old family harmonies, particularly those between Rosamond and her sister Kathleen, since the disparity in their incomes places them in separate social castes.

Questions of financial morality are important in the novel. Because St. Peter has been adamant in refusing to touch a penny of the wealth from Outland's invention, he is rankled to see Rosamond and her husband, Louis Marsellus, live so extravagantly on what they have not earned. Mrs. Crane, wife of a fellow professor, wants a share of the Outland money, since she is convinced that her husband's connection with the inventor entitles him to it; and she is prepared to institute a bitter and sordid court trial. The exploitation of Outland's tube works havoc among the St. Peter family and within the university faculty. On at least three occasions Cather reserves the emphatic position at chapter ends for comment. On the first the Professor, chancing to look up one evening on the physics building, feels a "sharp pain" like the heartache of Cather's middle-aged artists: "Was it for this the light in Outland's laboratory used to burn so far into the night!" On the second Kathleen, the more admirable of the sisters, reflects on the irony of Outland's effort: "Yes, and now he's all turned out chemicals and dollars and cents,

hasn't he?" Finally, the Professor ponders the burden placed upon
his conscience: "If Outland were here to-night he might say with
Mark Antony, *My fortunes have corrupted honest men.*"[26]

The Babbitt-like opening scene of the novel depicts the St. Peters'
dispute about whether a bathroom ought to be the most attractive
room in a house. The professor has known many people possessed
of great charm who had no bathroom at all, but he is overridden
by his partner's shrill argument, "If your country has contributed
one thing, at least, to civilization, why not have it?" By such attitudes the actors in the story are known. Tom Outland, whose
presence haunts the book, had rushed to Europe to die for a principle in comparison to which the commercial possibilities of his invention seemed trivial; he abandoned "the most important discovery of
his time to take care of itself." St. Peter, renouncing profit, explains
to Rosamond: "There can be no question of money between me and
Tom Outland." Kathleen's husband, Scott McGregor, is a writer of
some potential; but whatever true distinction he might have earned
is being lost through his profitable arrangement for writing a daily
"prose poem" for a syndicate:

> When your pocket is under-moneyed and your fancy is
> over-girled, you'll have to admit while you're cursing
> it, it's a mighty darned good old world.[27]

Once committed, Scott finds himself locked in economic chains. His
ambition to achieve "something very fine" is squandered in producing banalities.

The two sisters drift into vicious competition, and Rosamond,
being the wealthier, is always victorious. Her home and her furs
become banners of superiority. "Everybody knows she's rich,"
Kathleen tells her father, in tears; "why does she have to keep
rubbing it in?" On a shopping trip to Chicago, Rosamond indulges
in "an orgy of acquisition" that her father can equate only with
Napoleon's rape of the palaces of Italy. Moreover, the "new commercialism" works its poison on the university level. A demand that
education "show results" vulgarizes it in St. Peter's eyes. He works
to reverse the steady erosion of the sciences and humanities; even in
his classroom he plays the good soldier; like a Claude Wheeler
suddenly articulate, he delivers an impassioned lecture: "I don't
myself think much of science as a phase of human development. It
has given us a lot of ingenious toys; they take our attention away

from the real problems. . . . Science hasn't given us any new amazements, except of the superficial kind we get from witnessing dexterity and sleight-of-hand. It hasn't given us any richer pleasures, as the Renaissance did, nor any new sins—not one! . . . I don't think you help people by making their conduct of no importance—you impoverish them."[28] St. Peter challenges his students to provide a convincing answer for the question of the age: What has science done for man besides making him more comfortable?

Midway through the novel, Cather's dissection of the modern temper is rent to make room for "Tom Outland's Story," which occupies nearly a quarter of the novel. In St. Peter's lecture he informed his class that art and religion, in his thinking, were synonymous—"the same thing, in the end." The story of the Blue Mesa exists as an illustration of this belief. When Tom Outland, working as a Colorado cowboy, explores the mysterious and tantalizing rock that juts a thousand feet from the plain, he discovers there the abandoned cliff city, intact, as though one day its people had simply packed up what they could carry and had departed. Their abandoned dwellings speak of balance and unity, of an idea of order foreign to the modern welter; the village holds together symmetrically, with power. Even empty, it has significance, quietly "looking down into the canyon with the calmness of eternity." Harmony of architecture bespeaks a community at peace with itself: "One thing we knew about these people; they hadn't built their town in a hurry. Everything proved their patience and deliberation. . . . A people who had the hardihood to build there, and who lived day after day looking down upon such grandeur, who came and went by those hazardous trails, must have been, as we often told each other, a fine people."[29]

Father Duchene, of the local mission, guides Tom toward the same link between art and religion of which St. Peter spoke: "'I am inclined to think that your tribe were a superior people. Perhaps they were not so when they first came upon this mesa, but in an orderly and secure life they developed considerably the arts of peace. There is evidence on every hand that they lived for something more than food and shelter.'"[30] In clues left behind—the superior shapes and the decorative qualities of their water jars— Father Duchene locates the aspirations of the ancient people. From turkey bones and the remains of granaries, he traces their history as a provident tribe, subsisting on a meat and vegetable diet, establishing irrigated fields for corn, and domesticating sheep whose wool might be loomed and dyed with energies formerly devoted to the arts of war:

"I see them here, isolated, cut off from other tribes, working out their destiny, making their mesa more and more worthy to be a home for man, purifying life by religious ceremonies and observances. . . . Like you, I feel a reverence for this place. Wherever humanity has made that hardest of all starts and lifted itself out of mere brutality, is a sacred spot. Your people were cut off here without the influence of example or emulation, with no incentive but some natural yearning for order and security. They built themselves into this mesa and humanized it.'"[31]

The cliff dwellers, who are akin to Cather's artists, pursue the solitary way toward perfection. They are the first society, but not the last, through whom she explains herself by juxtaposing past with present.

Also like the artists, the ancient people do not prevail wholly against the pernicious. Hoping to preserve his find, Tom Outland, undertakes a trip to Washington; but he soon realized that neither his Congressman nor the Indian Commissioner has the slightest conception of what his discovery means; indeed no one has any genuine interest in hearing of it. After days of waiting in an outer lobby of the Smithsonian Institution, Tom is advised by a stenographer to invite an official to lunch, preferably to an expensive one at the Shoreham; in this fashion one commands a man's attention in the capital. Luncheon with an underling arranged, Outland finds his guest interested only in drinking a $5 bottle of Chateau d'Yquem and in reciting an account of the receptions he has attended. Nevertheless, Outland perseveres in order to gain a subsequent appointment with the Smithsonian's director. Proving more corrupt than his hirelings, this man "borrows" the choicest of Blue Mesa pottery for his personal collection. Tom is forced to understand that the overriding concern among the Institution's staff is the possibility of all-expense appointments to a forthcoming international exhibition. "They don't care much about dead and gone Indians," snaps his sympathetic stenographer. "What they do care about is going to Paris and getting another ribbon on their coats."[32]

Outland's depressing sojourn makes his return to the mesa particularly exhilarating: to stand atop the rock again "in a world above the world" and to inhale its rarified air are like "breathing the sun, breathing the colour of the sky." But this experience precedes his discovery that during his absence his partner has sold the cliff-dweller relics, complete to waterpots and mummies, to a German curio dealer who has already spirited the highly salable articles through Mexico to waiting ships. Tom protests: "'There never was any question of money with me, where this mesa and its people were concerned. They were something that had been preserved through the ages by a miracle, and handed on to you and me, two poor cow-punchers, rough and ignorant, but I thought we were men enough to keep a trust.' " His partner explains, nonplussed: " 'I didn't know you valued that stuff any different from anything else a fellow might run on to: a gold mine or a pocket of turquoise.' "[33]

The Professor's House is among Cather's most pessimistic books; it envisions no satisfactory explanation of the materialistic fever and proposes no cure for it. Where hope is gone, escape seems the only alternative. Like Mrs. Wheeler's finding cause for thanks in Claude's death, St. Peter finds himself relieved that Tom Outland has not lived to be caught by "the trap of worldly success." Those left behind face a bleak prospect, a life "without joy, without passionate griefs"; and he had never imagined that he might have to exist in this manner. For himself St. Peter manages no happy escape. The fine world of his mind is abrading under the world's pressures, and in one desperate moment suicide seems his escape. His stove is defective; his asphyxiation would be considered an accident. A tempting alternative—but the Professor is too stoical to accept it: "He had never learned to live without delight. And he would have to learn."

VI *What Is Love Worth?* My Mortal Enemy

That the thought of repeating herself was repellent to Cather is expressed in her books through a contempt for artists who are willing to do the same thing over and over again. Working on *The Professor's House* pleased her as an opportunity for doing something quite different, both in form and subject, and particularly because the book relied so little upon the western farm country with which the public tended to identify her. Her continuing effort to avoid Nebraska is evident in the slight but intense story—her briefest "novel"—that followed *The Professor's House*. In certain respects *My Mortal Enemy* is the converse of *My Ántonia:* rather than deifying one who genuinely elevates emotion above money, Cather undertakes the portrait of a woman who hoodwinks herself into marrying under the delusion that love is her first concern; but she learns, when she knows herself better, that her essential passion is for money.

Myra Driscoll is young and impetuous when she falls in love with Oswald Henshawe, whose qualities of "personal bravery, magnanimity, and a fine, generous way of doing things" suggest the youthful Captain Forrester of *A Lost Lady*. Unfortunately, Oswald is neither brilliant nor rich; and Myra's wealthy great-uncle, her guardian, opposes the marriage, understanding his niece's weakness for luxury, and threatens disinheritance. "It's better to be a stray dog in this world than a man without money," he warns her; "I've tried both ways, and I know. A poor man stinks, and God hates him."[34] But Myra elopes with Oswald, and her story is a chronicle of mounting regret.

Attributes of many Cather women combine in Myra, who is the unpleasant, grasping woman long in the background of Cather's novels; but in *My Mortal Enemy,* such a woman now comes to stage center. Myra Driscoll Henshawe has Marian Forrester's dependence upon "courtesy from people of gentle manners," just as she has Kitty Ayrshire's repugnance for life on anything but "very generous terms," a pair of attributes most easily sustained by money and position. Myra has neither of the latter, and she suffers grievously. She is, like Mrs. St. Peter, naturally snobbish; she is mad for "stables and a house and servants, and all that went with a carriage!"; but she lacks the private annuity that brought Mrs. St. Peter some of these luxuries. Myra—who is surely what Professor St. Peter had in mind when he dreaded "a woman who would always grow more exacting"—is proof of the distance Cather had come from her canonization of opera singers and pioneer women. Not merely is *My Mortal Enemy* a history of a "greedy, selfish, worldly woman" and the lust for luxury that is the root of her own great unhappiness, but it is also Cather's last direct thrust at the materialism rampaging throughout contemporary society.

The inadequacy of her husband's income might have impeded Myra's "insane ambition" to play lady bountiful, but she indulges her extravagance regardless of his economic status. The couple is perpetually on the brink of insolvency. She is first observed as she explains to an incredulous Oswald why his six brand-new dress shirts have gone to the janitor's son; they bulged slightly in front: "You shan't wear shirts that give you a bosom, not if we go to the poorhouse"—and the poorhouse is not a mere figure of speech but a real threat. Myra is next seen selecting a marvelous holly tree, "the queen of its companions," for a friend's Christmas gift. "That is naturally hers," she exclaims. "It's naturally the most extravagant," her husband rejoins. The shrug of his shoulders reveals his capitulation.[35]

When Myra inevitably regrets her marriage, she is too proud to admit she was wrong about herself; but her disenchantment grows as her attitudes regarding love and money become ever more cynical. Rather than prospering as Myra had anticipated, the Henshawes meet with ruinous reverses that force them to vacate their luxurious New York apartment. Loss of the wealthy, artistic—and insincere—acquaintances she has cultivated so assiduously is not an unexpected consequence, but for Myra it is a disaster. She sees her reverses as utter degradation. Eventually she comes to despise Oswald, who is the symbol now of her delusory emotions responsible for her elopement and disinheritance. At last, ill with cancer, she cries in desperation: "But why must it be like this? . . . Why must I die like this, alone with my mortal enemy?"[36]

Her cry of anguish completes Myra's confusion. Willing when young to put her faith in emotions, believing that money would follow love as day follows night, she has awakened gradually to a realization of being duped. Her feelings break to the surface in bitter words. When an artist friend seeks her approval of an expensive necklace purchased for his sweetheart, she is driven to suggest that "Love itself draws on a woman nearly all the bad luck in the world; why, for mercy's sake, add opals?" When she ran away with Oswald, Myra in her rashness had quit her great-uncle's house with nothing but her muff and a handbag, proudly disdaining possessions; but in discussing the romance of her artist friend with Nellie Birdseye, who narrates the novel, she reveals what life has taught her: "You send a handsome fellow like Ewan Gray to a fine girl like Esther, and it's Christmas eve, and they rise above us and the white world around us, and there isn't anybody, not a tramp on the park benches, that wouldn't wish them well—and very likely hell will come of it."[37] Of her own tarnished romance with Oswald, she sighs to Nellie, "Oh, if youth but knew! . . . It's been the ruin of us both. We've destroyed each other. I should have stayed with my uncle. It

was money I needed. We've thrown our lives away." As her resources fail, and with them her social position, the indispensability
of wealth becomes obsessive. Money is the world's one safeguard,
protective like a heavy warm cloak against inclement weather; "it
can buy one quiet, and some sort of dignity." Death comes as Myra
arrives at her great-uncle's philosophy: God hates a poor man.

The title of the novel cuts two ways. As Myra sees it, Oswald, em-
bodying the infatuation that cheated her of an inheritance, is her
mortal enemy. But her enemy resides equally within Myra herself
and is her gratuitous slavery to the things of this world. To equate
happiness with a generous income has been her misery, for Myra
never sank to actual destitution. Money, as always, was a relative
thing; and except in her own eyes, she was never truly poor. As a
sick and dying woman, she turns her malignance upon Oswald; yet
her spite may be taken also as self-indictment, for "violent natures
like hers sometimes turn against themselves . . . and all their idola-
tries." Dying, she at last is able to see herself plainly and with one
honest effort to give voice to her despair: "I was never satisfied. . . .
I am a greedy, selfish, worldly woman; I wanted success and a place
in the world."[38]

With *My Mortal Enemy* Cather had come a long distance from her
first novels, with their irrepressible heroines. The modern woman,
like the modern age, suffered by comparison with earlier models. It
was painful for Cather to contemplate the diminution of life that had
occurred—so painful that the present era, along with its Myra Dris-
colls, would henceforth be viewed only obliquely, from vantage
points strategically placed in the past.

VII   Mesas Encantadas: Death Comes for the Archbishop *and*
Shadows on the Rock

With *The Professor's House* and *My Mortal Enemy*, Willa Cather
confronted contemporary society head on for the last time in her
major works; for after these novels she turned to locales of the past.
There is a tendency to view this change as a withdrawal from life or
to call it Cather's retreat into sanctuary; but—without denying the
justification for such a view—her use of the past culminates her
long-standing preference. Because of the time lapse between her
experiences and their expression in books, she had always been
prone to using as her material events long-remembered and to contrast the life around her with older generations—twentieth-century

tendencies versus pioneer ideals, for example. In *One of Ours* the diminished second-generation Nebraskans exist within chastening shadows of heroic parents.

Use of a much older civilization as a standard of measurement began in Cather's short works such as "The Enchanted Bluff," was promoted to the status of a major incident in *The Song of the Lark*, and became a sizable, separate section of *The Professor's House*. In *Death Comes for the Archbishop*, the life of the past takes over entirely; and the present exists only insofar as one recognizes its implicit inferiority to aspects of a vanished glory. This change of emphasis accounts for the elegiac tone so readily detected in this novel and in *Shadows on the Rock*.

Cather's choice of a religious context is also not surprising, considering her preference for religious terminology in describing theories of art. Her artistic dedication, when it does not suggest espousal to art in sanctified wedlock, suggests membership in some religious order, a taking of "vows" to serve art and no other god. And the Outland section of *The Professor's House* adequately prepares for the exemplum of the past to unite with the art-religion concept and emerge, not as interpolation, but as the book itself. This synthesis occurs for the first time in *Death Comes for the Archbishop*.

In most Cather novels of the 1920s, the central actors are victimized: they threaten to drown in the murky currents of their time. But Cather now turns back to the indomitable hero. As Alexandra averts the corrosive greed of pioneer descendants and as Thea leaps over the traps into which weaker artists tumble, so Father Jean Marie Latour, avoiding the errors of his predecessors and refusing to compromise his aims, succeeds in establishing his great diocese from the ruins created by centuries of neglect of the Church in the Southwest. "The old mission churches are in ruins," says a Cardinal pondering the task; priests are few and without discipline, religious observances are nearly suspended, and concubinage is open and notorious. In a Roman garden a group of churchmen discuss the qualifications the new vicar must have—youth, health, zeal, intelligence—for he will be contending against savagery, ignorance, and political intrigue. He must have a rage for order; it must come first and must be as dear to him as life itself.

The candidate selected is Latour, a French Jesuit; and his trial is not so very different from that of one attempting to scale the frozen heights of art. His will be no easy life, for the Southwest "will drink up his youth and strength as it does the rain." Fortunately Father Latour proves equal to the challenge. Thea Kronborg's ability to smell out her natural enemies is in him as well, and he identifies a trio as the chief rogues: Padre Gallegos of Albuquerque, Padre Martinez of Taos, and Padre Lucero of Arroyo Hondo. Gallegos, a slave to physical luxury, spends his nights in dancing and playing poker, and his table groans with choice foods and wines. Martinez has surrendered to the flesh; in any settlement one might find his children, and his aim is to eradicate the celibate clergy. Lucero, the mendacious priest of Arroyo Hondo, lusts for money, having found avarice the single passion extending into old age even stronger and sweeter than in youth.

Latour wages, therefore, a holy war of purification. The priests of his diocese arrange in two ranks; and whether they are friend or foe, trusty captain or despicable traitor, depends on whether they live "for the people or upon the people." Latour pictures his diocese as a blighted tree; and amputation of the rotten limbs is its only cure. In his work he has good help in Father Joseph Vaillant, a vicar much like himself and a priest whose contrast with Gallegos, Martinez, and Lucero could not be more pronounced. Vaillant, "most truly spiritual," is fully disciplined for the fray, faithful, uncomplaining, and frugal. Renouncing possession (he claims only his mule Contento), he reminds Latour of a saint of the early Church; and nothing less than a saint is required to help Latour in his task.

Dual strands of narrative—Latour's and Vaillant's—mesh well as Cather exploits her favorite technique, contrast: she pits the serenity of the agrico-nomad Indian society against the turbulent commercialism of an emerging American influence. Father Vaillant, transferred from New Mexico to gold-rush Colorado, reflects upon the Indian capacity for traversing a land "without disturbing anything," for passing like a fish through water or a bird through air. A contrast with modern rapacity, though no more than hinted at, is always present: "They seemed to have none of the European's desire to 'master' nature, to arrange and re-create. They spent their ingenuity in the other direction; in accommodating themselves to the scene in which they found themselves. . . . It was as if the great country were asleep, and they wished to carry on their lives without awakening it; or as if the spirits of earth and air and water were things not to antagonize and arouse."[39] The Indian hunted but did not slaughter; he used the rivers and the forest but did not ravage them; and knowing the value of water, he conserved it. There was no desecration of the environment. Although the novel is limited in time to mid-nineteenth century, it manages to speak with a voice of outrage against the modern craze for leaving one's marks on the land, for altering it past all recognition, even to the removal of mountains, as if the ruination of a landscape were the ultimate test of human endeavor.

When Vaillant travels to the boom area where "nobody would stick a shovel into the earth for anything less than gold," he plunges into a lawless society that is already producing the first ugly signs of industrial expansion "where guile and trickery and honourable ambition all struggled together." The remainder of his life is devoted to combatting elements that brutalize life and to replacing them with humanizing forces. His integrity is measured by the account of his funeral, held out of doors under canvas because no building in Denver would contain the crowds of mourners. Vaillant's story reinforces the major theme, for he wars against a materialism that respects no person or institution. Even in the Church, and perhaps there above all, the holy war demands continual vigilance by fighters free of personal ambition but with a youthful vigor sufficient to turn back the vices and all the vanities that warp the life of the spirit.

Death Comes for the Archbishop tells of the Indians of Ácoma, who built for themselves a highly ordered society adapted to the barren rock on which they chose to live. The mesa in turn served to preserve that society by isolating it from forces incapable of improving it but prone to upsetting its delicate balance. Beneath the mesa ran a secret spring that provided drinking water, the life of the colony. And if a foreign element entered the mesa, irritating it like a speck in the eye, it was plucked out—eradicated as the tyrannous Fray Baltazar had been, for he, according to legend, was flung from the top of the mesa.

The prospect of a small group's cooperating to perfect a humane way of life in sheltered isolation intrigued Willa Cather sufficiently for it to became the central motif for *Shadows on the Rock*, in which the mesa becomes the rock of Quebec, which is settled not by Indians but by eighteenth-century French colonists. Cather's friend Edith Lewis says that *Shadows on the Rock* owes its origins largely to chance; for when visiting Quebec, Cather was startled to encounter an authentic bit of old France transplanted intact to America. Her visit occurred not long after publication of *Death Comes for the Archbishop,* and the author, still under the influence of the Southwest, at once recognized the Quebec parallel and made her decision to write about it. She had described the New Mexican mesas as resembling cathedrals, and here was another rock, beside running water, that with its buildings took on the outlines of an immense chapel.

What the French pioneers bring with them to Quebec is not a mere replica of life in France but an idealized version of it—a heightened one because it is safely removed from the evils threatening Europe. In seventeenth-century France life could be very unpleasant, even for the noble classes, who were likely to become immeshed in court intrigue whether they sought to or not. Corruption was the rule, and a discerning man might smell revolt in the air even at the time the émigrés withdrew. The wealth of France was being sunk into the pleasure palace at Versailles; rich men ran in a squirrel cage, ruining themselves in a rivalry for magnificence and display. The homeland had become a Gallic version of pre-Latour American Southwest.

The émigrés find their solution in a completely new beginning. Euclide Auclair, the apothecary, expresses the prevailing horror when he reminds his daughter, "The Law is to protect property, and it thinks too much of property. A couple of brass pots, an old saddle, are reckoned worth more than a poor man's life." Canada poses hardships unimaginable in Paris, but it releases the settlers from materialistic shackles that at home could not be stricken off except by blood. Auclair considers himself fortunate to have thirty-five hundred miles of water insulating his family not merely from present corruption but from future chaos.

Interest centers upon the culture being established in Quebec and the measures taken to assure its preservation. Striking similarities tie the book to *O Pioneers!,* for once again Cather deals with a first generation of pioneer immigrants to America, the taming of a wild land, and confidence in one's adventure. The great diocese of *Death Comes for the Archbishop* encompasses thousands of miles, but Quebec is isolated upon its single fortress rock, moated by two rivers, thickly hemmed in by forest. Within this restricted place, the action is static while attention focuses upon the citizens' construction of a new life.

The book concentrates upon the household of Auclair. His life devoted to his patron, Count de Frontenac, Auclair has moved his shop—drugs, fixtures, and furnishings—to America after the Count's appointment as governor of Quebec. Mme. Auclair, who is determined that her family traditions shall not succumb to the wilderness, brings the customs, artifacts, and—particularly—the recipes that undergird a civilized life. To her, a traditional cuisine serves as a bulwark against savagery; a pot of breakfast chocolate can symbolize a mode of life. Mme. Auclair comes to an early death, but her daughter, Cécile, is trained to recognize that civilization is a fragile package to be passed with care from one generation to the next. On her deathbed she gives instructions: "'The sheets must be changed every two weeks but do not try to have them washed in the winter. I have brought linen enough to last the winter through. . . . You will see that your father's whole happiness depends on order and regularity, and you will come to feel a pride in it. Without order our lives would be disgusting, like those of the poor savages. At home, in France, we have learned to do all these things in the best way . . . and that it why we are called the most civilized people in Europe.'"[40]

Alexandra Bergson's mother brought from Sweden much of the same regularity; on the plains of Nebraska she insisted that berries be gathered to preserve for winter use, just as at her old home. She and Mme. Auclair are together in understanding that civilization does not characterize human society automatically but must be renewed, tended like a sacred fire: "The sense of 'our way,'—that was what she longed to leave with her daughter. She wanted to believe that when she herself was lying in this rude Canadian earth, life would go on almost unchanged . . . that the proprieties would be observed, all the little shades of feeling which made the common fine."[41] The mother's fidelity, bequeathed successfully to Cécile, makes the apothecary's home a bastion of the civilized. Food is a primary symbol; the Auclair attitude is that of Father Latour when he explained the care taken with his soup by pointing out that it was not one man's recipe but the end result of long refinement, each bowl representing a thousand years of history.

Auclair's is not a typical household; it is the best, just as Alexandra's was the best farm, and Thea's the perfectly utilized voice. The Auclairs' idealized state contrasts with homes in which the loss of tradition has reduced human beings to an animal existence. When

Cécile visits the Harnois family on the Île d'Orléans, she finds the food coarse, carelessly prepared, unpleasantly served. The Harnois' failure of management comes as an ugly shock—their bread is ruined with too much lard, and no one seems to mind; but such details portend barbarism. Mme. Harnois prepares breakfast in her night cap because she has not taken time to arrange her hair—a trifle, but a significant one. At night Cécile finds herself in bed with four Harnois daughters dressed in the same chemises they have played in all day and whose legs are splashed with mud and the blood of mosquito bites. Soiled sheets go unchanged for weeks; and, in the dark, unable to sleep, Cécile recalls "how her mother had always made everything at home beautiful, just as here everything about cooking, eating, sleeping, living seemed repulsive." In the end the trivial, individual act determines whether or not one would make something fine out of his existence: "These coppers, big and little, these brooms and clouts and brushes, were tools; and with them one made, not shoes or cabinet-work, but life itself. One made a climate within a climate; one made days,—the complexion, the special fla- vour, the special happiness of each day as it passed; one made life."[42]

Cather's art-religion synthesis continues. Churches and nun- neries abound; and the city itself, with its structures arranged in ascending layers up the rocky slopes, appears to be one massive church. Members of religious orders play significant roles. Bishop Laval, having given away his possessions, his revenues, and his lands, lives in "naked poverty." The martyr Noël Chabanel chooses to live among the savage Hurons. Jeanne Le Ber, daughter of Mon- treal's richest merchant, withdraws from material comfort to cloister herself in a barren cell whose four walls enclose the world wherein she prays and knits for the poor; when her confessor urges her to leave her cell at least for recreation in the open air, she protests, "Ah, mon père, ma chambre est mon paradis terrestre."

These ascetics are introduced not to augment a "churchy" atmo- sphere or to intensify a theme of pious resignation but to comple- ment scenes in the Auclair household. In both the domestic and religious spheres, an unending effort is maintained in order to edge the direction of man away from the material and toward the ideal. In Quebec the compass turns in the only direction in which Cather senses hope: "When an adventurer carries his gods with him into a remote and savage country, the colony he founds will, from the beginning, have graces, traditions, riches of the mind and spirit. Its history will shine with bright incidents, slight, perhaps, but precious."[43]

VIII *Diabolus in Virginia:* Sapphira and the Slave Girl

Cather's distaste for possession, wealth, and status as employed in the modern world—and her horror of a life disoriented by them—is expressed vigorously in her later writing. Minor works published during the period of her religious novels reinforce the austerity that had become the passion of her maturity. A long story of 1925, "Uncle Valentine," follows a composer as he leaves the wealthy wife whose money has smothered his talent; and the story is an angry one. In a bitter tirade Valentine Ramsey characterizes this woman, Janet Oglethorpe: "'She's a common, energetic, close fisted little tradeswoman, who ought to be keeping a shop and doing people out of their eyeteeth. She thinks, day and night, about common, trivial, worthless things. She bargains in her sleep.'"[44]

For five years, Valentine has trailed after Janet on her world travels; and he has lived in a paralyzing atmosphere—one common, mean, and coarse. His experience with invincible thing-worship is what Cather most dreaded about the postwar world. In any direct contest the idealistic seemed doomed to go down before a cultural Gresham's law according to which a wave of vulgarity was to overwhelm all that was fine. Withdrawal, if not the only answer or necessarily the best, was an effective remedy; and with that trust Valentine returns to Pittsburgh. The welcome influence of native hills and forests makes work possible once again, and he produces the songs that later establish his fame. Then Janet follows, and she purchases adjoining acreage. Too soon "the sound of the mason's tools rang out clear across the cut between the two hills; even in Valentine's study one could not escape it." As Janet's new palace rises, Valentine knows he is trapped: "Everything about her's bunk, except her damned money. That's a fact, and it's got me.'"

Attempting a second escape—to Paris—Valentine dies under the wheels of a motor truck, Cather's symbol for the mechanized anarchy that deals a death blow to the ordered life so vital to art. Her narrative ends on a note of triumph for the enterprises of the world's Janet Oglethorpes: "The wave of industrial expansion swept down that valley, and roaring mills belch their black smoke up to the heights where those lovely houses used to stand. . . . The roses of song and the roses of memory, they are the only ones that last."[45]

But even in the beleaguered cities of America—steadily more lockstepped, their populations cloned from a single drab model, all "living the same lives, striving for the same things, thinking the same thoughts,"—one might happen upon rare individuals who are deliberately out of step with the times. Cather's story "Double Birthday" (1929) is in praise of one such family. Old Doctor Engelhardt has retired from active practice, having reached the decision that music is more important to him than pill dispensing; and his son Albert has followed his example. Since the two live on accumulated principal, their estate dwindles, and they take up residence in a dilapidated house with the remnants of fine possessions left from more prosperous days. But the Doctor has no regrets, nor does Albert: "he had had the best of it; he had gone a-Maying while it was May. This solid comfort, this iron-bound security, didn't appeal to him much. These massive houses, after all, held nothing but the heavy domestic routine; all the frictions and jealousies and discontents of family life. . . . Money? Oh, yes, he would like to have some, but not what went with it."[46]

Rather than being despised by their friends of other days, the Engelhardts are held in awe as a symbol of possibility, particularly by a neighbor, Judge Hammersley, who inwardly is skeptical "of what is called success in the world to-day." His daughter shares his pessimism, for she has seen too many fine things vanish. The coming generation is to be pitied: "'They seem to me coarse and bitter. There's nothing wonderful left for them, poor things; the war destroyed it all. . . . All houses are like hotels; nothing left to cherish.'"[47] The improvident example set by the Engelhardts fails, however, to draw recruits; the Hammersleys admire but lack courage to follow. But for those who swim against the tide, Cather offers something close to canonization.

Prominent on Cather's litany of modern saints is the farmer-hero of "Neighbour Rosicky," a first-rate story that has often been anthologized since its appearance in the 1932 collection *Obscure Destinies*. This short story is a coda to *My Ántonia* and reputedly derives from the same materials. A Bohemian boy in search of a fruitful life, Anton Rosicky immigrates to London at eighteen, but finding sweatshop life there unspeakably mean, he makes his way to New York. For five years he works as a tailor; then he feels the old compulsion to run. His awakening occurs on a holiday afternoon when the city is drained of its usual population and can be observed clearly, with time for reflection: "Those blank buildings, without the stream of life pouring through them, were like empty jails. It struck young Rosicky that this was the trouble with big cities; they built you in from the earth itself, cemented you away from any contact with the ground."[48] Rosicky finds his salvation in Nebraska, married to a Czech girl on the Divide. Here he farms his land with equanimity, rainy year or dry; and his thought centers totally on his family's welfare.

Rosicky's is the familiar Cather retreat from conditions too powerful to resist. Cities have become impossible; "all the foulness and misery and brutality of your neighbours was part of your life." Under Nebraska's open skies a man is comparatively free. The rest of the world is already at arm's length, and if need be, Rosicky can post his fields to keep meanness at a distance; good fences will make good neighbors. Rosicky is not unrelated to the recluses of Quebec who withdraw from the midst of life into solitary cells for their souls' sake, and a good deal of their attitude toward possession appears in his belief that "you couldn't enjoy your life and put it into the bank, too." To Rosicky, avarice is nothing less than living death. When his neighbors take pride in marketing their rich cream, themselves existing upon the leftover skim milk, his gorge rises. "I'd rather put some colour into my children's faces than put money into the bank," his wife declares. Rosicky agrees.[49]

Rephrased, the leitmotif of Anton Rosicky spills over into *Lucy Gayheart*: "Some people's lives are affected by what happens to their person or their property; but for others fate is what happens to their feelings and their thoughts— that and nothing more,"[50] Lucy "never seemed to think about money. When she had any, she spent it gaily. She refused to be poor in spirit." She shares this outlook with her friend Clement Sabastian, a famous musician and a man to whom wealth is no more than a means toward a conveniently generous life. But Lucy's sister, Pauline, has ordered the family orchard chopped down to make room for a profitable onion field, a self-damning action comparable to Ivy Peters' draining of the Forrester marsh. Pauline considers it Lucy's familial duty to marry Harry Gordon, the richest boy in Haverford. Harry, while not obnoxious, would do better to marry Pauline, since his penuriousness matches hers. He has acquired a trait by which his family is known, the "instinctive unwastefulness" that made the Gordons rich to begin with.

Of the two men, Lucy quite naturally prefers Sebastian: "Harry

Gordon was rich, to be sure; he owned carriages and blooded horses, sleighs and guns, and he had his clothes made in Chicago. But his things stood out, and weren't a part of himself. His overcoats were harsh to touch, his hats were stiff . . . in a big city he took on a certain self-importance, as if he were afraid of being ignored in the crowd whereas Sebastian . . . had a simplicity that must come from having lived a great deal and mastered a great deal."[51] The ludicrousness of marrying Harry Gordon strikes Lucy during a visit to the Chicago Art Institute when Harry faults an impressionistic canvas for inaccurately drawn figures.

"I don't think it matters," Lucy suggests; "I think some are meant to represent objects, and others are meant to express a kind of feeling merely, and then accuracy doesn't matter."

"But anatomy is a fact," persists her suitor, "and facts are at the bottom of everything."

Lucy can answer quietly only, "Are they, Harry? I'm not so sure."[52]

The pair is voicing a basic incompatibility and Lucy, who lives by emotion, feels leaden, "as if he had brought all his physical force, his big well-kept body to ridicule something that had no body, that was a faith, an ardour."

Antipathy toward the notion of property characterized Willa Cather's fiction beginning with her earliest experiment, when she wrote of that prototype of all her barbarians, Antone Sadelack, trekking to town to sell his father's violin bow on the morning of his funeral. Like her major heroine, the one most resembling herself, Thea Kronborg, Cather has creative hate for her natural enemies— those unable to employ money generously or wisely, with natures too vulnerable to the tyranny of ownership. Thus comes her homage to those abjuring possession altogether, the unacquisitive Indian, the religious ascetic. To renounce the things of this world became in time her *magnum summum*, the best because the hardest, the most difficult but the most rewarding.

Buried deep in all of Cather's books hides an implicit damnation of capitalism itself; it never surfaces into any outright confrontation because of the author's horror of polemic literature (and because of her rearing in a money environment—she, as well as any other, being the product of her time). But, hide it as she will, her denunciation of capitalist flaws crops out in thrusts against prime symbols:

cash and property. Individual ownership and the right of a titleholder to do what he pleases, no matter how low his taste or motivation, are a form of anarchy deadly to the sense of order she saw as the basis of humane existence. This anarchy lies behind the most dastardly deeds in her fiction, such as Ivy Peters' despoiling the marshland. But until her final novel Cather's distrust of property as such was a sword lodged in stone.

Until her final years Cather did not feel ready to use in fiction the Virginia environment from which she was removed in childhood. Yet hidden in that past, a subject well worth treating was identified before it became too late. The dark secret of Virginia was slavery, the ultimate crime of private ownership. This issue, on which the Cathers of Winchester had sundered and which in time had led to the Nebraska move, became the subject of *Sapphira and the Slave Girl*. The story of a family broken on the wheel of slavery was something Cather might tell, for its polemic quality could be diminished by its location in the historical past.

The Colbert family includes Henry, the miller; his wife Sapphira; their daughter Rachel Blake. Sapphira, the slave owner, is born to a society erected upon the fact of ownership and dedicated to its divine ordination. Cather presents Sapphira as "an entirely self-centered" woman of iron determination, and her right to do with her slaves what she pleases is to her a sacred privilege not to be abridged. Henry Colbert, his mind troubled since marriage, is in turmoil when his Bible yields him no unequivocal condemnation of slavery. And slavery is a barrier that blocks Rachel from her mother; but Negro placidity disturbs her as much as Sapphira's ownership—the slaves accept the fact of their bondage much too readily. This paradox troubles Rachel until she finds an answer for herself: Sapphira believes in slavery, the slaves themselves seem to believe in it, "But it ain't right." In the background other voices are heard; for Sapphira's relatives form a solid front to guard their property. Against them stand the Bywater family and various Quakers. One senses the earth rumble as the Abolitionist crusade of the 1850s begins.

Sapphira is no *Uncle Tom's Cabin*, but the effects of slavery on the human spirit are graphically presented. One meets Jezebel, betrayed by members of her own tribe turned slave hunter. She has seen her father brained, her brothers cut down in an attempt to protect her, and her village reduced to ashes. The brutal ocean passage of the slave ship is sketched, as are the methods by which Jezebel's spirit was broken. One meets Till, Sapphira's house servant, who is arbitrarily wed to a "capon man" as an imposed birth-control measure. One meets particularly the Colbert family itself, crippled by dissension.

The opening scene involves a quarrel in which Sapphira, determined to barter her slave girl Nancy to a neighbor, is angered by her husband's curt refusal: "We don't sell our people." That he will not put his signature to the deed is an affront to her ownership. Rachel also resists the sale: "A feeling long smothered had blazed up in her—had become a conviction. She had never heard the thing said before, never put into words. It was the *owning* that was wrong, the relation itself, no matter how convenient or agreeable it might be for master or servant. She had always known it was wrong. It was the thing that made her unhappy at home, and came between her and her mother!"[53]

The Civil War and its campaigns play no part in Cather's narrative, but within the miller's family a rebellion wages, with Nancy the focal point. In her anger Sapphira is ready to have her head turned by malicious gossip that links her husband's opposition to the sale of Nancy with the possibility that his interest in her is sexual. In order to circumvent Henry's opposition, she devises her own means of ridding herself of the girl, who is now regarded as a threat to her marriage. Nancy will be exposed to their guest, a dissolute young cousin, with rape the anticipated outcome. Then the mores would demand Nancy's expulsion from the place. Knowledge of this plot prompts Rachel to action. With her father's help she succeeds in smuggling Nancy through the underground railroad to Canada, an act of defiance that severs all ties between mother and daughter and that prefigures the divisions soon to accompany the outbreak of war itself.

In Willa Cather's final baring of materialistic evil, she dispenses altogether with personal ambition and uses in *Sapphira*—as in her religious novels—heroes who place principle above self, society above family. Significantly she returns to the source of thematic statement that had first served her four decades earlier in "The Professor's Commencement": Henry Colbert, readying for the night, takes down his well-thumbed volume of John Bunyan's *Holy War* and opens it to a passage depicting the town of Mansoul after Diabolus has smashed through her gates: " 'Also things began to grow scarce in Mansoul: now the things that her soul lusted after were departing from her. Upon all her pleasant things there was a blast, and a burning instead of a beauty. Wrinkles now, and some shews of the shadow of death, were upon the inhabitants of Mansoul. And now, O how glad would Mansoul have been to enjoyed quietness and satisfaction of mind, though joined with the meanest condition in the world.'"[54] Rather than leave the book on this depressing note, Henry reads farther in passages describing Mansoul as being retrieved by Prince Emmanuel. The thought that evil would not triumph was reassuring.

In this manner—obliquely, through another analogue of the past—Willa Cather came to the final unbosoming of her hope that the holy war for modern America might somehow be won against powerful material infiltration—if only the Ear Gate of Mansoul were sentried by trusty captains.

CHAPTER 5

The Voyage Perilous:
Cather and Creativity

> All this question of art is just another
> version of Bunyan's siege of the town of
> Mansoul.
>
> —Willa Cather, 1896

I First Principles

TO scan writings from Willa Cather's collegiate years is to witness her in the process of achieving a serviceable concept of art and the methods of attaining it. She evidently avoided any formal inquiry into criticism, learning instead by observation and by doing. Between 1893 and 1896—to consider only her work for the Lincoln newspapers—she wrote some 250 critical pieces. Typically these involve a response to an artist's performance; and generalizing from there, the review serves as a medium for thinking aloud. Whether pleased with a performance or dissatisfied, the young Cather worked always to isolate principles basic to her response. After 1920 the mature author from time to time wrote formal essays in criticism; but "The Novel Démeublé" and "On Escapism," which are among the better known, contain scarcely a single idea not thought out and set down in print a quarter of a century earlier. The later essays refine her concepts, but Cather's view of art can best be seen taking shape in her first eager reviews.

For a responsive and inquiring mind to read books, attend plays, hear concerts, and visit exhibits is to learn; for if great art is difficult to define, it can be readily experienced; and the experience is unmistakable. Cather belongs with the intuitive critics for whom art remains "an awesome mystery." Had she heard Emily Dickinson say that one knew poetry by the effect it produced—something akin to knowing that the top of one's head has been taken off—she would have been bound to approve, since her own theories rest upon similar recognitions. One knows when the lightning has struck, whether he can define it or not; and Cather's responses to singers and actors are of this type. What is strongly felt at once—the emotion of the instant—the critic rushes to get down on paper before it hardens into an opinion or freezes into a deduction.[1] One's spontaneous judgment is best precisely because it is truest.

Cather was aware when a performance left her chilled; but when one stirred her as deeply as Clara Morris' 1893 *Camille*, she could only call it "perfect." The language offered no other more satisfactory adjectives for, "when we find a perfect individual creation, we accept it as unquestioningly as we accept nature's work, and upon it we build a whole philosophy of art."[2] Cather built no formal philosophy, but she did manage to derive guiding principles that served, virtually unaltered, for half a century as a guide in her own writing; and these can help us achieve a greater understanding of the eternally elusive creative process.

Her most basic belief held that art, perhaps the highest of human callings, emanated from "an Artist . . . of such insatiate love of beauty that He takes all forces, all space, all time to fill them with His universes of beauty."[3] Two strands join in this statement: the mystical origin of genius and its mission—to create beauty. Art at its zenith lies beyond human power to do or to comprehend; thus did Cather speak of "heights beyond which even art cannot rise" decades before she quoted Geraldine Farrar (in terms undoubtedly her own, not the singer's) regarding the unattainability of the frozen peaks. In the 1890s Cather had written that Duse's performances touched the "icy heights," the "stainless heights" beyond mortal capacity.

Out of the divine, then, from "somewhere out of the region of the vast unknown" arrive the actors, poets, singers, and painters who have received the Call. The finger of God is laid upon them, and they are not like common men; to quote a phrase that Cather borrowed from Henry James to use and re-use, they partake of "the madness of art." The muse might be courted, but it never could be compelled by artists, those "strange beings . . . doomed and destined" to create. The world's function is to provide necessaries, in return for which the artists "give us our dreams." For the ordinary human being, the enjoyment of art consists in "watching a man give back what God put into him."[4]

Considering such views, one is not surprised to find Cather couching her thoughts in religious terminology, speaking of Duse's

art, for example, as her "consecration, her religion, her martyr-
dom," and of her progress among the theaters as a pilgrimage "from
shrine to shrine to perform some religious worship." Similar examples characterize the Cather reviews. Because Mary Anderson considers the art of acting "a stepping stone, not an altar," her audiences find her performances cold. To write a short story is to design
a spire, but the novelist is required to build a cathedral. No artist
can expect to reach "the temple of fame" by walking the Rialto in
creased trousers, and the life of art provides for no deathbed repen-
tences: "It takes a whole long life not only of faith but of works to
give an artist salvation and immortality." All of these words were
written, these principles established, decades before Cather caused
Godfrey St. Peter to pronounce that Art and Religion are synonymous.[5]

In March 1896, after Cather had graduated from the university
and had spent a year free-lancing and just prior to her departure for
Pittsburgh, she summarized her stand on the special position of art:

Great thoughts are not uncommon things, they are the property of the
multitude. Great emotions even are not so rare, they belong to youth and
strength the world over. Art is not thought or emotion, but expression,
expression, always expression. To keep an idea living, intact, tinged with all
its original feeling, its original mood, preserving in it all the ecstasy which
attended its birth, to keep it so all the way from the brain to the hand and
transfer it on paper a living thing with color, odor, sound, life all in it, that is
what art means, that is the greatest of all the gifts of the gods. And that is the
voyage perilous, and between those two ports more has been lost than all
the yawning caverns of the sea have ever swallowed.[6]

II *Forsaking All Others*

"Expression, expression, always expression"—to achieve it places
an awesome responsibility upon the artist. Chosen, possessed of
genius, forever set apart, "his very strength lies in the fact that his
needs, desires and life are different from those of every man on
earth." Creative power, never synonymous with mere talent nor
acquired through effort, is the unique evidence that "every true
artist is in the hands of a higher power than himself, that he cannot
do what he will, but because he must." His creative work becomes
his single purpose, single hope. To achieve some perfection, in
whatever field, is his chief need; and to reach this end the only safe
course for an author "is to cling close to the skirts of his art, forsaking
all others, and keep unto her as long as they two shall live."[7]

That devotion to art should be expressed in terms of a holy wed-lock is no mere figure of speech, for to Cather art had become a religious mission. Hence Duse, always her model for the actress, "has worn the motley as if it were a nun's hood." For Kipling, concerned over his wife's reaction to the climate of his chosen resi-dence, Cather offered editorial advice; he must remember that he was married to his works long before meeting Mrs. Kipling. Many men might have married her, but only one might write *Soldiers Three*. Cather quoted him his own lines, "He travels the fastest who travels alone." For an artist the single life is preferable. Problems of the married pervade Cather's early reviews, all declaring the poor mixing qualities of domestic and artistic life. Most succinct is her observation that "married nightingales seldom sing."[8]

An interdiction on marriage supports in part the need for artistic isolation, but friends make claims also; the fewer one has, therefore, the better. Some acquaintances tend to be officious, but all demand interest on their investment in one. No artist should expect love, popularity, or "happiness" in the ordinary sense. Dedication is equated with loneliness, but such loneliness is the freedom to follow one's star undistracted. It provides an artist both solitude and liber-ty, the two wings of art. To "live" and to "create" become antitheti-cal; to attempt both is to build simultaneously in brick and marble: "Now, when a man has this double task of living and working laid upon him, one or the other must suffer in proportion as the tasks are great and he is weak. If his work suffers we hoot him and say he is an imposter; if his life suffers we damn him and say he is degenerate, but we hoard his achievements away in our treasuries of beauty."[9]

To retreat to a quiet place of one's own held an attraction for Cather long before Miss Jewett advised it. In 1894, on the occasion of Robert Louis Stevenson's death, Cather wrote of him as self-marooned on his South Seas island:

He was safely out of the civilization that kills more authors than it stimu-lates. Safely out of the reach of literary friends and advisors, of the futile blame and barren praise of the public, of tempting offers from the holiday magazines, of literary dinners and musicales and high teas. Free to change and polish and recast his work until it was without a blemish, until weari-ness and the sense within him told him to stay his hand. That, perhaps, is why he has left us a few perfect books rather than a great many brilliant shallow ones.[10]

In his retreat Stevenson found the order and harmony that Cather sensed in the shards and architecture left by the cliff dwellers and that she expressed when she wrote of Thea Kronborg's visit to Panther Canyon. The same qualities undergird both *Death Comes for the Archbishop* and *Shadows on the Rock* in which the arts of living are borne into isolated outposts, preserved there, cherished, and refined.

To be great, an artist must transcend the trivial. None but the purest of motives may be served, and the first essential is a lofty conception elevated by high artistic sincerity. If an artist loves all human things, if "some great belief" stimulates him, then he may succeed. Conversely, the "begetter of all evil" is insincerity. "Soul" becomes a word much used when Cather reaches for an explanation of the ultimate contact point between the vision of perfection and the written approximation of it. Whatever is to be understood by soul, defined as art's supreme virtue, Cather links it with the tranquil, the honest, and the orderly. The soul's polar opposition to madness, chaos, confusion is why the writer can profit by removing himself from a civilization that "is always beating about our ears and muddling our brains" and why he sometimes needs "solitude and the desert, which Balzac said was 'God without mankind.' "[11]

III *The Writer's Craft*

Only when a writer's mind is filled and his eye dazzled by a great situation is he ready to attempt expression of his idea. Even then, a truly artful expression can be approached only through collaborative effort between "man's most perfect work and God's divinest mood." Genius without craft is little; craft is nothing without genius; but should the two join—as when a great natural voice is developed by superior training—accomplishment knows no limit. For the writer a knowledge of his craft is indispensable, and when Cather approaches this subject, the mists of her theory fade to reveal hard specifics.

To say that the end of art is the creation of life, as Cather believed it to be, is to state an ideal; but the closer the duplication of nature, the higher the art. At its peak, surmounting human limitation, art would become life itself. Humans must be content with approximations in which one struggles toward a sense of reality. For Cather this means not the "realism" emerging in the 1890s but a convincing impression of life, which is something else again.

The purposes to be served by art must be understood; as must, equally, the purposes with which art has little to do. Art does not teach morals, nor serve as a channel of information, nor propagandize for any cause. While these aims may involve "art" of a sort, this art is of a lower degree surely, and those serving such ends are by definition minor. Does God ever moralize through nature? Cather delivers a resounding "No." The creation is its own excuse for being: "His laws are the laws of beauty and all the natural forces work together to produce it. The nightingale's song is not moral; it is perfectly pagan in its unrestrained passion. The Mediterranean at noonday is not moral, the forests of the Ganges have no sermons in them."[12] When Edwin Royle's play *Friends* appeared in Lincoln, Cather found it praiseworthy purely because it was without evident purpose, without pretensions of morality or immorality; the play was simply a good one. Emotion was meant to be exalted, not analyzed, she felt; and surely it was not to be denigrated. *Passion, beauty, emotion*—these became Cather's passwords.

Much might be learned from the wide variety of reading a reviewer encountered. The "unfortunate tendency" of female novelists to instruct was a flaw that Cather was determined to avoid, for one might learn as readily from the imperfect as from the flawless. Plotting, for instance, so tempting and so easily overdone, could be a trap leading the unwary to place action above truth. For this reason mystery stories rarely make for lasting satisfaction—their actions and their characters seemed, to Cather, "as absurd as the puppets of a Punch and Judy show."[13] Pathos, counterfeit of the genuine, was to be approached with caution. Certain facts and conditions that are in themselves pathetic—poverty, loneliness, death—do not lead automatically to great fiction. And, concerning the prevalence of local color, Cather could only express doubt that by itself it "ever gave any real greatness to any man."

Gingerly she picked her way through the excesses, the fashions, and the fads—the wrong turns of her day: "Melodramatic literature has been overdone until we are weary of blood and passion, realism has been pushed to its last limit until we are sick of the barnyard and gutter, and as for the weird and fantastic—heavens, is there one more nerve left in us that has not been jangled and jarred by these craftsmen of the impossible? *Vive la bizarrerie!* is the literary watchword; we have studies in color, studies in environment, studies in heredity, studies in sex, studies in anything but common sense. Anything that is odd, unheard of, unnatural 'goes.' "[14]

Mrs. Stowe's *Uncle Tom's Cabin*—its thesis hung round its neck

like an albatross, its mediocrity expected, but its genuine badness
unanticipated—she found "exaggerated, overdrawn, abounding in
facts but lacking in truth."

This statement was another way of indicating Willa Cather's distinction between the actual and the true, which were not always the
same. The overwrought senses of Oscar Wilde and his esthetes
added up, for Cather, to a kind of insanity; but "realism"—what
today is called "naturalism"—seemed the most grevious offender of
all. Setting out to reproduce life in photographic detail, it succeeded, insofar as Cather could tell, only in giving back an extremely unlifelike effect. Emile Zola was the principal culprit, but
Henrik Ibsen was not far behind him. She compared Zola's work to a
granite bull dug from the ruins of Nineveh, massive but lacking "the
impress of a human soul." He wrote not literature but social science.
To be persistently sad, as she found the majority of Scotch novelists
to be, was as narrow as to be persistently frivolous; "sadness in six
entrees with a funeral for dessert" was not to her taste. The "realists" seemed off balance, as if forgetting that the world contains
pleasure gardens as surely as graveyards, sonnets as well as epi-
taphs.[15]

Fortunately, Cather thought, analytical realism had limits. Extended "until it reaches the ugly skeleton of things, there it must
stop," the human mind refusing to be dragged farther. When that
time arrived, then the reversal would come; and realism would be
replaced by romance. The romantic appealed to Cather during the
1890s, for in it she saw escape from present excesses and hope for
the future: "Some fine day there will be a grand exodus from the
prisons and alleys, the hospitals and lazarettos whither realism has
dragged us. Then, in fiction at least, we shall have poetry and
beauty and gladness without end, bold deeds and fair women and all
things that are worth while."[16]

Cather's notion of romance, one must add, was not that simplistic
view that places it at a polar removal from realism. To her, "romance" affirmed the supremacy of imagination over reportage; it
concerned not the surface, but the universals supporting the surface. Romance in Hawthorne's sense and use of the term was a
method of revealing truth without being tied to photography; in her
eyes Stevenson and James were the great contemporary romanti-
cists. But literary labels are notoriously unhelpful; and the terms
romanticism, *realism*, and *naturalism* have perhaps created more

problems than they have solved. Adherents of each say its aim is Truth—indeed, Hamlin Garland found it useful to coin an entirely new term, *veritism*, to say precisely that—but *what* Truth and *whose* Truth is not so easily said. H. W. Boynton in 1918 classed Cather as a realist, describing her method as "that of the higher realism; it rests not at all upon the machinery of dramatic action which is so right and essential for romance," and he was correct in noting her conscious subordination of surface activity.[17]

Edward and Lillian Bloom categorize her within the realism of Stuart Sherman, which implies a representation of life grounded upon a theory of human conduct and which stands in an antagonistic opposition to naturalism.[18] Bernice Slote considers Cather a passionate idealist, while René Rapin is convinced that she should be labeled a classicist because her "innate romanticism is checked by realism and both are made subservient to an ardent love of life and a respect for truth"; because she studies problems of wide and permanent interest; and because of the purity of her style.[19] H. L. Mencken championed Cather as a modern exemplum of the realist whose mark was "intellectual honesty" in treating his materials—the power to see things as they are with an eye unclouded by sentimentality or illusion. Because of Mencken's belief that the intrinsic interest of a novel lay in "some one man's effort to master his fate," he was bound to like Cather's work because this effort was her generic theme.[20]

To complicate classification of her works and interpretation of her statements, Cather at the same time that she was castigating the new realism was herself writing stories that dwelt on the black side of life; "A Wagner Matinée" and "Paul's Case" display more affinity with literary naturalism than with any traditional concept of the romantic or even of Howellsian realism. Although she extolled the imaginative, her definition of imagination is all-important; for rather than meaning an ability "to weave pretty stories out of nothing," imagination conveyed to her "a response to what is going on—a sensitiveness to which outside things appeal" and was an amalgam of sympathy and observation.[21]

Despite Cather's apparent distaste for the subject matter and philosophy characteristic of literary naturalism, she could not sufficiently praise the first substantial American example of that genre, Frank Norris' *McTeague*. The novel seemed mature and compact, the product of a writer of "power, imagination and literary skill." The poet and the uncompromising realist seemed joined in a book that circumvented the literary abuses of the age and at the same time created that "illusion of life" marking only the highest fictional art:

Mr. Norris has dispensed with the conventional symbols that have crept into art, with the trite, half-truths and circumlocutions, and got back to the physical basis of things. He has abjured tea-table psychology and the analysis of figures in the carpet and subtle dissections of intellectual impotencies, and the diverting game of words and the whole literature of the nerves. He is big and warm and sometimes brutal, and the strength of the soil comes up to him with very little loss in the transmission. His art strikes deep down into the roots of life and the foundations of Things as They Are—not as we tell each other they are at the tea-table.[22]

Cather's review of *McTeague* praises exactly those qualities she attempts to achieve when her own novels find their natural subject matter. "He sees things freshly," she wrote, "as though they had not been seen before, and describes them with singular directness and vividness, not with morbid acuteness, with a large, wholesome joy of life." No more pertinent comment could have been made upon the Cather of the Nebraska novels, and one does in fact find the same points made in reviews of *O Pioneers!* and *My Ántonia.* Her aim always was to create literature about people as she knew them, one that would balance hope against despair and match the power of conditions with a triumph of the will. And she felt that the hope for American literature lay in so doing: "If there were one man who could write of the American common people, the people on whom the burden of labor rests, who plant the corn and cut the wheat and drive the drays and mine the coal and forge the iron and move the world, then there might be some hope for a literature of and from the American people. But so far our men who write of the people at all write of trusts and strikes and man-devouring railroads, of the mere condition of labor and not of men at all."[23] She searched, in short, not for sociology, economics, psychology, or political science in masquerade, but for literature.

IV   *Throwing Out the Furniture*

In Cather's opinion the most useful principle—the single principle if only one might be named—crucial to the writer's craft is selectivity. On every level, from choice of subject to use of form to individual word, the selection process is necessary. Because of her conviction that the worth of material is variable, Cather could not agree with Whitman that the ocean's imperious waves and the fly specks on the wall were equally worthy. She felt that Whitman wrote "reckless rhapsodies" whose veneration for all things, good and bad, sublime and ridiculous, was charming and very nearly convincing; but in the end, they proved his weakness and left him a poet "with no literary ethics at all beyond those of nature." Lacking finer discriminations, he enjoyed everything with boyish enthusiasm—and never grew up.[24]

Cather's own experiences made her acutely aware of the distinction between the journalist who trains himself to write equally well whatever the subject and the creative artist who can do his best only with subjects of deep personal involvement. Although she entered journalism herself in the hope that it might open doors to another career, she soon recanted, branding it "the vandalism of literature." The newspaper in particular lowered art to the level of a trade; for, devouring intellect and talent, it returned only colloquial gossip. Journalism, she declaimed in a bitter moment: "is written by machines, set by machines, and read by machines. No man can write long for any journal in this country without for the most part losing that precious thing called style. Newspapers have no style and want none. A newspaper writer should have no more individuality than those clicking iron machines that throw the type together."[25] Cather believed that the artist, who cannot afford to scribble impetuously, must avoid the temptation to get things on paper too early. Only those subjects that are above the hubbub of life and that persist in demanding expression may be heeded; and by this artistic reticence the true, the genuine, and the significant prevail.

Cather's essay "The Novel Démeublé" calls for a novel stripped of excess event and language, summarizing her doctrine of simplicity. A remark of the elder Dumas—that to make a play, he required but four walls, two people, and one passion—she found in youth, often repeated in her reviews and essays, and used as nucleus. Deletion of the extraneous and the redundant helped a writer both to intensify and to simplify his work. Cather took note of the multitude of literary sins committed in the name of description, whose value to her appeared to be "in inverse ratio to the length."

Most books, if boiled down to half their bulk, she felt, would lose none of their beauty and would also be made more readable. Mrs.

Humphry Ward's novels made an ideal object lesson; for blessed with considerable descriptive powers but tyrannized by her own facility, Mrs. Ward particularized ad infinitum to the detriment of her fiction. Writers were tempted by a false analogy with landscape painters who filled every square inch of their canvases with detail. Such a method was self-defeating in fiction, Cather felt, for the eye could take in a canvas at a single glance and create its own instant impression by selecting from what was offered. The printed page, on the other hand, must be read particular by particular, and excess detail "is likely to overtask the memory somewhat and blur the ultimate clearness of the picture."[26]

To present information is not the major aim of fiction; the artist should suggest the character of a place or an atmosphere. For this reason, "a few masterly strokes suffice," and one's ability is measured by what is felt to be on the page without actually being there. "It is a hard job," Cather said, "to do a portrait in ink without getting too much description."[27] All art, whether singing, writing, or sculpting, must simplify. For Cather that seemed the entire process, and she used painting for an illustration of it: "Millet did hundreds of sketches of peasants sowing grain, some of them very complicated, but when he came to paint 'The Sower,' the composition is so simple that it seems inevitable. It was probably the hundred sketches that went before that made the picture what it finally became—a process of simplifying all the time—of sacrificing many things that were in themselves interesting and pleasing, and all the time getting closer to the one thing—It."[28]

The French short story, with its knack for grasping the heart of a situation, served as a literary model. The French had learned that one critical episode was sufficient to tell about a life or to analyze a character, and even their longer novels typically possessed the "conciseness and directness" of the short story. "I like a book where you do one thing," Cather said in 1925, speaking of her determination that the portrait of Marian Forrester should dominate A Lost Lady; but she might have referred to almost any of her works, and she surely spoke of literature in general. Every novel, every story in finished form should resemble the painter's final composition and be the distillation of many other stories sacrificed to it: "You must save the thing that is most precious to you, even if you have saved it at the cost of a number of conventional things."[29]

V *No Sentimental Tricks*

The artist conducts a perpetual search for ideal form. After 1910 Cather was fond of referring to the ancient potters of the Southwest who shaped and decorated their jars not to increase the game supply or to promote tribal security but to satisfy esthetic impulses—to create something fine in itself. Cather's notion of form—like Whitman's—was organic. Each story, like a living thing, must be free to seek its own inherent shape; and the story will do so if guided by character and theme, for these *are* the story. An artist is not content to impose a standard pattern, like a sonnet form imposed artificially upon verse that strains for something else. Cather had learned a lesson with *Alexander's Bridge*, in which the error of excessive attention paid to plot had caused disappointment in the result; in her next work she was determined "not to 'write' at all" but to let her materials dictate their own shape.

This decision is explained in Cather's 1913 review of Arnold Bennett's *Milestones*, a play she admired for its construction which was so unobtrusive that "the click of its machinery" was never heard. Avoiding the traditional sentimental tricks of plotting, Bennett included "no 'big scenes' artificially brought about for their dramatic effectiveness, no overheard conversations, no accidental meetings or unlikely coincidences." Instead, he allowed the "inherent vigor" of his theme to prevail; and he did so rightly, Cather was convinced, for a powerful idea "is like a spiral spring; once released, it will go its length without prodding." Even more vital to his play's success was Bennett's acknowledgment that "the real excitement" of literary art is not the order of events but living, breathing people. Bennett avoided brilliant dialogue in favor of homely, commonplace speech; but his people lived and were intensely dramatic "because of the situations that lie behind them. And the situations are dramatic, not in themselves, but because one is interested in the characters concerned in them. All good plays begin with the author's power of creating character. If his people are real enough and interesting enough, anything that happens to them is interesting."[30]

Alert to methods for best allowing her own characters and themes to express themselves, Cather took cues from the other arts. Fond of music all her life, she once told Fanny Butcher she could see "no reason why one cannot write a novel as a composer writes a symphony."[31] Richard Giannone's *Music in Willa Cather's Fiction* describes this impulse to build in the manner of musical themes, including her free admission that *The Professor's House*, with its tripartite design based upon contrast, was intended as an adaptation of sonata form. At times, painting served her in the same way.

In 1921 Latrobe Carroll heard Cather describe the procedure she was attempting with *A Lost Lady*, which was to follow the lengthy and detailed *One of Ours* but was to be radically different in shape. As much of herself as possible was to be eliminated; she would analyze, observe, and describe as frugally as possible. The constructive principle would be the juxtaposition of people and things; they would tell their own story, so rendering authorial comment superfluous: "Just as if I put here on the table a green vase, and beside it a yellow orange. Now, those two things affect each other. Side by side, they produce a reaction which neither of them will produce alone. Why should I try to say anything clever, or by any colorful rhetoric detract attention from those two objects, the relation they have to each other and the effect they have upon each other? I want the reader to see the orange and the vase—beyond that, *I* am out of it. Mere cleverness must go."[32]

Prior to writing *The Professor's House*, Cather had visited an exhibition of Dutch genre painters; and she was particularly interested in Vermeer's placid interiors with their calm, secure ambiénce and subtle coloration. One feature of his composition that intrigued her was his use of windows—open windows bringing into these interiors a view of all outdoors, often a highly detailed landscape that both complemented and contrasted with the enclosed room of the canvas. Thus emboldened, she proceeded to "Tom Outland's Story," inserted it centrally in her novel, and compared it to an open window that would "let in the fresh air that blew off the Blue Mesa" and establish its own contrast with the hauling and the pulling of modern civilization.

One expects the principle of juxtaposition to operate in Cather's story collections, where separate tales serve to develop aspects of the major theme that binds all together. She produced only three collections in her lifetime, and her selectivity in determining what would be saved assured their unity. Each story becomes a "panel" in a larger work, but that the same principle operates in her novels is less often recognized. *The Professor's House* has its Outland Story; *O Pioneers!* combines three stories in many ways separate unto themselves; *Death Comes for the Archbishop* consists of nine books, largely separate entities yet also coordinate panels in a single story. Individual portions—"Doña Isabella" and "The Legend of Fray Baltazar"—are easily excerptable by themselves; and one, "December Night," has been printed alone, as has "Tom Outland's Story."

In these panels the short-story quality Cather strove for, the ability of the critical episode to serve all, is realized. While *Death Comes for the Archbishop* also holds together by virtue of larger unifying principles of character, setting, and theme, the book (Cather called it not a novel but a narrative) has much of the epigrammatic sense she admired in French writing. As early as 1895, Cather had asked, "What is *Les Misérables* but a series of perfect short stories?" In the three decades following, her juxtapositional principle became more or less instinctive. Going once again to the painter's art, Cather attributed her book's overall form to the inspiration of Puvis de Chavannes' frescoes recording the life of Saint Geneviève, which she had seen in the Pantheon of Paris. In *Death Comes for the Archbishop*, she hoped her literary art would duplicate something approaching their static mural quality, "something without accent, with none of the artificial elements of composition."

This aim is highly reminiscent of Whitman and his refusal to allow decorative curtains, however rich, to hang between him and his reader. Despite her reluctance to admire Whitman, Cather resembles him strongly in this respect and in his call for organic form; and she may be taken as one example of Whitman's pervasive influence upon the direction of American writing. His call for the honest treatment of integrally American subjects and his confidence in the divine afflatus that touched genius also are basic to Willa Cather's concept of art and the craft of writing.

CHAPTER 6

Trumpets of Fame: Cather's Career

> . . . the day of an artist's greatness is by
> no means over when she leaves the stage. In
> a certain sense it has only begun. Then she
> has the authority of a career that is complete,
> a work that is finished, a destiny that is fulfilled.
> —Willa Cather, 1895

I *World's Fair Palaces*

FROM the time she entered college—and probably earlier—
Willa Cather courted fame;[1] but she sought no quick or cheap
success, for she had encountered enough flash-in-the-pan notoriety
in stage life not to mistake anyone's publicity for real acclaim. What
she hoped for was the renown owed the genuine artists of her fiction, those who maintained faith in their genius and brought it to
fulfillment through hard work, a lifetime of dedication to high aims,
complete sincerity, and full control of one's craft. By practicing
herself what she preached for others, she hoped to arrive in due
time. Art's divergent paths, said Latrobe Carroll, are giving the
public what it demands or making one's work so fine the public will
demand it; and Cather consistently decided in favor of fine work.

Just what constitutes "fine work" is not always easy to know; even
Cather, in finding her way to it, followed a number of blind trails
and embarked on many false starts. But she thought, as has been
noted, that success has a good deal to do with locating one's natural
material, submitting to it, and then writing to the best of one's
ability out of a basic and universal emotion. To live deeply, to feel
deeply, to know as much as possible of the human condition—these
are essential; but in the end, what one records of the experience of

living is what really counts—art being, as she had phrased it, "expression, expression, always expression."

Cather once described the history of literature's resemblance to a stroll through the grounds of a defunct world's fair. One sees palaces of former grandeur with stucco peeling and chipped; jerry-built villages, stripped of flashy veneer, reduced to studs and broken plasterboard; artificial lakes reverting to original swamp. Time took its inexorable toll. Her own ambition was to build something quite different, something that would endure.[2] Her aim was that of all art, and perhaps of life—to defeat time itself. Neither size nor imposing façade would serve, but only the artifact crafted supremely well from the finest material· "Let who will cavil of carving cherry stones, it is the perfect thing, however small, that outlasts the ages wherein faulty epics are entombed without memorial."[3] Her strongest wish was comparable to that of Robert Frost, who said that his life was spent in lodging a few poems where they would be hard to get rid of. She hoped, like Stevenson, to leave behind her "a few perfect books."

By way of assuring this ambition as her legacy, Cather attempted to manipulate the hand of fate. Whenever possible, she directed attention away from herself and toward her writing—but only toward the best of her writing. At any time from the mid-1920s to the mid-1930s, when Cather's popularity was at its highest, a volume of hitherto uncollected stories would have been assured of substantial sales. Yet only one collection appeared, *Obscure Destinies*, and its three stories were new ones. Cather's aim was clarified when the 1937-38 Library Edition of her works appeared, an edition for which Cather provided final revisions of her stories and novels, deleted unsatisfactory passages, and added explanatory prefaces. Significantly, for this "complete" edition Cather ignored dozens of stories she had published in magazines between the 1890s and the 1930s. By her silence she rejected these works and—so far as she was able—consigned them to oblivion. This aim to be known only by her best had a long history, for soon after 1910, when Elizabeth Sergeant let her know that she had located a copy of *April Twilights*, Cather expressed disappointment at having her apprentice work brought to light. She told Sergeant that she thought she had purchased all the extant copies of her poetry and had sunk them in a lake.[4]

Cather hoped to influence her long-range reputation not only through what she chose to make permanent in her collected works but also through what she forbade in the stipulations of her will. She strongly suspected that translations of literary works into other media never redound to the enhancement of the originals; and apparently her disappointment with the film version of *A Lost Lady* proved to be decisive, for in her will she prohibited any further adaptation of her works into motion pictures. At the same time she refused to allow her books to be adapted for radio, television, or other media. Presumably in order to assure a focus on herself as writer rather than as personality, Cather interdicted any publication of her letters. Fanny Butcher, recipient of many notes from Cather, has expressed her personal disappointment at this restriction, saying, "If Willa Cather's other letters resembled those she wrote to me, they could do nothing but add to her stature as a great writer and as a rare human being, both of which she was."[5] Cather disagreed, obviously, and during her lifetime made definite efforts to prevent her letters from coming to light, even going so far as to burn those returned to her upon the death of her closest correspondent, Isabelle McClung Hambourg. Elizabeth Sergeant has recorded the "chill of regret and dismay" she experienced when she learned that those bundles of letters were being methodically incinerated.

Willa Cather once said that if she could get a carpenter to make her some good bookcases, she would have as much respect for him as she had for those whose books she wanted to put on their shelves.[6] She felt that "something well made" represented the goal of human effort, and she described her *Lost Lady* in artisan's terms as a thin miniature painted on ivory, insisting that there was "nothing but that portrait." What she said of Poe in 1895 seems to have become ingrained as she aged: "The man is nothing . . . . The work is everything."[7] Just as Cather herself was as intrigued by Poe's life as she was by the idealistic life pattern discernible in the pottery shards she picked up at Mesa Verde, so has curiosity concerning the writer herself grown as interest in Cather's fiction survives. Although her letters cannot yet be published, they have been preserved where possible; her early stories have been republished as copyrights have expired; and her extensive journalism, much of it pseudonymous, has been reprinted.

One envisions Cather's ambition becoming an idée fixe during those evenings in Lincoln's Funke Theater where she, a green nineteen, was already an official critic for an important local newspaper.

And those players who shuttled across the continent by rail, eager to entertain in any city, town, or hamlet with so much as on over-the-hardware-store opera house—they ranged from mediocre to magnificent, and each played his part in opening for Cather the secrets of art and of fame. She saw talents wasted on trivial materials, and she sensed flint striking fire in a genuine evocation of life—and both events told her things of importance.

Cather had no singing voice and certainly no talent for the professional stage, but she could do one thing well—write. But who had ever heard of a writer coming out of Nebraska's wasteland? Insanity and suicides, yes. But a writer, particularly a great one, seemed highly unlikely. Then the example of Olga Nethersole intervened. Being British, Nethersole was expected to be cold and undemonstrative; all British were. But the actress's passionate perfor-mance in *Camille* and the rave notices she garnered for it proved to Cather that nationality was not invariably fatal. Nationality or environment might limit one's physique, character, temperament, even one's talent, but could it effectively influence one's genius? She thought not. With perseverence a gifted child from a small prairie town south of the Platte might yet find her way up the literary Everest. And then—"The trumpets of fame, when they are loud enough, are sometimes heard even in Lincoln."[8]

II   *Mind Over Nebraska: 1910–1920*

The trumpets, what there were of them, were muted until 1913. Willa Cather had built a certain following with her occasional magazine stories; her poems had caused no stir at all; and *The Troll Garden*, while admired, was a thing of the past by 1913. *Alexander's Bridge* had been given a good but by no means sensational reception; the astute H. L. Mencken, who called it "promising," said that if it showed the influence of Edith Wharton throughout, Cather had at least had the intelligence to choose a good model.[9]

But *O Pioneers!* announced a wholly different Willa Cather, one who had found her literary bearings; and critics were convinced of her talent by her evocation of the pioneer era in Nebraska. Even more reassuring to her was their admiration for her rendering of character, that mainspring of fiction. Her novel told a good story, but it went considerably beyond mere story quality to "something finer. . . . a direct, human tale of love and struggle and attain-ment," as the *New York Times* put it. A "power without strain" had been achieved by her simple treatment of an intense situation. Her preoccupation with formal symmetry abandoned, she had used an episodic structure that the *Bookman* called "a series of separate scenes with so slight cohesion that a rude touch might almost be expected to shatter it." Most reviewers felt, in brief, that few American novels in recent years had been so impressive.[10]

In 1915 *The Song of the Lark* drew a cool appraisal from some critics who disapproved of the more detailed method Cather had adopted and found her book "too long and too heavily burdened with details," its inner fire "smothered" by an extended portrayal of an opera singer's routine. Yet those detecting flaws found Cather's accomplishment in other directions truly fine. The concept of struggle and the convincing manner of Thea Kronborg's rise made the novel unusual; there had been many stories of operatic stars, but most were laughably artificial. Most found the highlight of the book to be its characters. Frederick Tabor Cooper was one of many who felt that characterization was perhaps Cather's chief strength as a novelist, and he closed his review in the *Bookman* on that note: "She has created a group of real persons; she takes us into their homes and makes us share in their joys and sorrows, with a quickening sympathy such as we give to our friends in the real world. And that is a gift that is perhaps quite as rare as a genius for plot-building."[11]

Critics were beginning to use the word *art* not merely because in this novel the life of the artist was thematic but because America was witnessing in Willa Cather the emergence of a native artist. H. L. Mencken, then on the rise but by no means yet the influential critic of later years, was on the lookout for writers he could champion as uniquely American. Already the chief booster of Theodore Dreiser, he now declared that Cather with *The Song of the Lark* had unquestionably stepped into "the small class of American novelists who are seriously to be reckoned with."[12]

Awareness of the Cather presence was general by 1918. She had pleased, even if there was still some caviling and a lingering doubt about her significance. Her next book would clearly be a touchstone, and fortunately *My Ántonia* turned out to be a masterwork that confirmed all her promise; the mists of doubt evaporated. No question about it, said H. W. Boynton, "Miss Cather is an accomplished artist." Those preoccupied with identifying native talent heaved a sigh of relief, for in her third major novel since *Alex-*

ander's Bridge, Cather had established that she owed nothing to Europe; she was ours alone—-finished, mature, and as nearly perfect as one might wish. "Here at last," announced Randolph Bourne in the *Dial,* " is an American novel, redolent of the Western prairie, that our most irritated and exacting preconceptions can be content with."[13] Practically no dissent from this view was printed.

The surge of interest in Cather extended to her style, of which reviewers had written in glowing terms. Boynton attributed her success with Ántonia's unorthodox story chiefly to method; the novel was like a painting in which no stroke is superflous or wrongly emphasized. Randolph Bourne found the secret of the Cather style to be its flawless candor, a naive charm that seemed artless until it was realized that "no spontaneous narrative could possible have the clean pertinence and grace which this story has." "Purity" and "quiet beauty" were typical summations.

Mencken, confident all along of Cather's capabilities, was naturally delighted; and he declared in his best Menckenese his joy that somehow, under "the swathings of balder-dash, the surface of numbskullery and illusion, the tawdry stuff of Middle Western Kultur," Cather had hunted out some genuine human beings and presented them in a novel "sound, delicate, penetrating, brilliant, charming." To those possessing a copy of *My Ántonia,* he issued a simple directive: "Don't give this away!"[14]

Cather's debut into fame was noted in volumes concerning American fiction, the first being Grant Overton's *The Women who Make our Novels,* issued late in 1918. A literary reporter rather than critic, Overton compiled information about all American female novelists of importance or popularity; but he did not prognosticate which of them, if any, might continue to be read fifty years hence. The order of his chapters was accidental and therefore meaningless, Willa Cather is sandwiched between one Grace S. Richmond, whose books were said to sell "faster than the books of any other American writer," and Clara Louise Burnham, author of "twenty-six books which have sold a half million copies." The thirteen pages Overton granted Cather are devoted largely to a biographical sketch (not always noted for accuracy) and to a summary of her achievement, drawn from reviews; these cover her work from *Alexander's Bridge,* which might have been written by Mrs. Wharton, through the indisputably personal triumph of *My Ántonia.* Overton's judgments, reflecting a cross section of others' evaluations, emphasize the significance of Cather's early western experience, her controlled accessibility to it, her fidelity to character, and the esthetic delight furnished by her method.

III *"Go Read Miss Cather"*: The 1920s

Every writer who is recognized in his lifetime knows a time when the cheering rings loudest, and for Willa Cather this period was the 1920s. Referred to as a novelist—as distinguished from a woman novelist—and as a major voice, she swiftly attracted an audience that eagerly anticipated each new book and purchased it in large numbers. Moreover, the criticism of her work assumed a new significance. When a review copy of *Alexander's Bridge* had arrived in the Chicago *Evening Post* office in 1912, Floyd Dell had given it as one of an armload of excess books to a girl who had stepped in off the street after mustering courage to beg for a chance as a reviewer. The girl later made a name for herself as Fanny Butcher; but at that time she was lucky to get even a semi-pseudonymous "F. B." attached to her review. After 1920, however, the most famous critics on the magazines reserved Cather for themselves and discussed her work in essays rather than in portmanteau reviews, and their names were prominently appended. When Cather was now compared with Mrs. Wharton, it was generally to her advantage, not Mrs. Wharton's; for she was thought to be not only equal to any American novelist but also superior to most.

Cather's books were now committed to the young firm of Alfred A. Knopf, and what few stories became available to the magazines were highly sought. Mencken said that his partner, George Jean Nathan, read "Scandal" in the *Century* with "envious rage" to think that their own *Smart Set* had not garnered it as it had "Coming, Eden Bower!" Both stories, the latter retitled "Coming, Aphrodite!" appeared in *Youth and the Bright Medusa* with which Cather successfully opened the new decade. This collection was followed by *One of Ours*, a disappointment that invited disparagement. The key to criticism of the novel is that those praising it blindly tend to speak in hollow generalities: "a thing apart," "a creation of artistry," "nobly epic," "epical dignity," "high-water mark." Those seeing the book as a failure attack it on the basis of more specific evidence, most often declaring that the second-half disaster results from Cather's lack of control over the battlefield scenes; they feel that she uses the war less to solve Claude's dilemma than to dispose of him and his problem conveniently. The *Nation* invited readers to a Hobson's choice between artistic self-deception or conscious intellectual abdication on Cather's part; and a young Edmund Wilson, evidently taking his first look at Cather's work, wondered aloud whether Mencken might have been mistaken in deciding that Willa Cather was a great novelist. But Robert Morss Lovett was certain that to everyone who knew "those boys" who fought in France, the book would have an immediate appeal that went "beyond words"; and he was correct, for the book sold exceedingly well and was awarded the Pulitzer Prize.[15]

In 1923 came *A Lost Lady*, which has been appraised as either the finest thing Cather ever wrote or the weakest; but the immediate reaction was heavily favorable. The book was regarded as a brilliant recovery; and Heywood Broun, for one, heaved a sigh of relief for Cather "back from the war safe and sound." *A Lost Lady*, based upon another memory of the early days in Nebraska, identified Willa Cather even more closely in reader's minds with her western materials, and this association bothered her considerably. Even in *One of Ours* the Nebraska section was what was praised and remembered. To be linked exclusively with the rural West rubbed disconcertingly against her conviction that local color by itself could never bring greatness. She had always before her the the example of Miss Jewett, who to Cather was a superb writer; but she was lodged in literary history as minor, as a regional writer and figure.

Harassment was to be expected on this score; for instance, Sidney Howard located the great lack of *One of Ours* in Cather's failure to recognize war for "the big bowwow stuff that it is," and his advice was that henceforth Cather "stick to her own farms and farmer folk." Such remarks bit sharply; and Cather, in turning to her new novel, very carefully explained that, however much she loved the West, she hoped not to be connected with any one region. She made it clear that readers could expect little of the West in *The Professor's House*. To use one setting all the time was quite like planting a field with corn season after season, Cather told Flora Merrill in an interview: "I believe in rotation of crops. If the public ties me down to the cornfield too much, I'm afraid I'll leave that scene entirely."[16]

That *The Professor's House* was different did not go unnoticed, for Henry Seidel Canby considered it to be a more innovative novel than even *O Pioneers!* had been. But the difference, for many, did not make the book better than Cather's previous work. Joseph

Wood Krutch headed his review simply "Second Best"; other critics made references to "loose ends," several employed the word "disappointment," and Moses Harper inquired whether it was really best for Cather to be always so sane, steady, and controlled. A. Hamilton Gibbs thought it not too much to say that "Tom Outland's Story" was better realized than the main narrative because the tale was "so much more simple and dramatic, so much more real." But invariably, whether a reviewer leaned pro or con, his notice was composed in the context of increasing Cather prestige; and if a novel was not all one might have anticipated, it was because it had been measured against the perfection of which she was thought capable.

My Mortal Enemy, which was almost too brief to be considered a novel, did little to influence Cather's reputation except to focus increased attention upon her style—a "cool, firm" method that steadily evoked admiration. When *Death Comes for the Archbishop* appeared in 1927, even the small group of dissenters from Cather's general chorus of praise agreed as to its stylistic merits, even though there was puzzlement over whether the new work fell within the novelistic range, strictly interpreted. D. F. Gilman, writing for the Boston *Transcript,* was straightforward: "In the first place, this is not a novel. In the second place, it is one of the most superb pieces of literary endeavor this reviewer has ever read, regardless of language or nation." L. W. Dodd found the book a staggering attempt serenely and triumphantly carried through, and Robert Morss Lovett pronounced it the equal in every way of Cather's "unquestionable masterpiece" *My Ántonia* and a book destined for classic status.

In the estimation of the public, readers and critics alike, Willa Cather had come into her own. Across the Atlantic Hugh Walpole in 1922 conducted a poll that placed Cather among the six most important living American writers; and the next year he listed her in a personal estimate among the five writers he most admired. In 1925–26 the *London Mercury,* discussing the Americans thought most worthy of notice, ranked Cather with Dreiser, Frost, Joseph Hergesheimer, E. A. Robinson, and Wharton. At home, when the *Literary Digest* published opinions of thirty-three magazine editors and publishers' advisors regarding the leading writers to have emerged within the decade ending in 1922, Hergesheimer led, followed by O'Neill and Sherwood Anderson, and Cather was in fourth place. But in the 1929 critics' poll conducted by Stalnaker and Eggen and reported in the *English Journal,* Cather was rated as the top novelist in the nation, for the overwhelming success of *Death Comes for the Archbishop* was incontrovertible evidence of her brilliance.[17]

The 1920s were the years for comprehensive summations, supposedly tentative, no one knowing what direction Cather's writing might take. But since they coincided with the height—and the end—of her prolific years, they came close to being definitive appraisals of her contribution. Most found it a time for homage; and among those offering major essays or chapters in literary volumes were Thomas Beer, Percy H. Boynton, Henry Seidel Canby, Elizabeth Drew, Sinclair Lewis, H. L. Mencken, Lloyd Morris, Burton Rascoe, Elizabeth Shepley Sergeant, Stuart Sherman, Carl Van Doren, Edward Wagenknecht, Rebecca West, and T. K. Whipple.

The words *art* and *classic* were used in these critiques with some abandon, and Rebecca West combined them in 1927 to achieve the title for her long essay, "The Classic Artist." In answer to the question as to whether or not an artist could exist in the United States, T. K. Whipple said it was necessary only to "Go read Miss Cather." She was often interviewed regarding her life and her books; she was photographed and sketched; and—the ultimate flattery—she was caricatured, as she described it, as G. K. Chesterton *sans* mustache. In Nebraska the trumpets of fame sounded loudly. The women of Omaha raised money to commission a portrait of Cather by Leon Bakst and, with due ceremony, hung it in the public library.

IV "Good Prose is Not Enough": The 1930s

The next decade opened with the publication of René Rapin's *Willa Cather*, the first of many volumes devoted to estimating her achievement. Based necessarily upon incomplete information and researched without the author's cooperation, Rapin's book attempted a comprehensive survey of Cather's life and work, and it used once again the label *classical*. It was premature, Rapin confessed, to attempt any really final appreciation of an author who was possibly only in mid-career; and while he was ready to pronounce her the creator of works truly great and enduring, he was not so rash as to anticipate whether the curve of Cather's reputation might tend up or down.

The curve, as it happened, went down. Cather turned fifty-seven in 1930, and her writing not only declined in volume but rarely managed to equal her previous standards of quality. She had to ride

on the strength of former accomplishment. Friendly reviewers—
and most were—found themselves uneasily admiring *Shadows on
the Rock* more for its art than for its substance. The writing was
superb, as expected, but the book appeared thin, undramatic, and,
if one were not kindly disposed, dull. *Obscure Destinies* more
nearly approximated vintage Cather, particularly for "Neighbour
Rosicky"; but hopes went down again with *Lucy Gayheart* and were
recouped only in part by Cather's final novel, *Sapphira and the
Slave Girl.*

One group in the literary world made Cather a special target. The
national depression fostered new critics who were uncommitted to
her work; some believed that literature must reflect the Marxist
principle of class struggle; many favored fiction as a tool of social
reform; and all searched for a novel highly involved with the current
scene. If a literary thesis were unmistakable and politically correct,
a favorable reception for the work was assured. Antagonism was not
directed at Cather alone; and, altogether, the change in attitudes
and in expectations was as much a revolution within criticism itself
as anything else; for the newer critics accused the older ones of
artificially supporting "fatigued writers . . . for whom the crisis has
obviously been too much." In this spirit, Robert Cantwell announced "the lamentable collapse of a number of those writers who,
only a few years ago, were being hailed as the creators of masterpieces and the leaders of American culture . . . whose latest books
have revealed their inability to deal with the emotional and practical
problems of the contemporary world in even the most elementary
terms."[18]

The attack upon Cather was led by Granville Hicks, who used his
review of *Shadows on the Rock* to propose that she was "a minor
artist"—no more than a brilliant local colorist; to be exact, she was of
the caliber of Sarah Orne Jewett. Particularly in the current scene,
he suggested, it took stern stuff to make a novelist; and Cather's flaw
had always been an unserviceable softness. Hicks charged her with
use of description for its own sake; and, with some sense of outrage,
he noted that Cather's later books, "with no apologies and to no
other purpose," devoted themselves to recreating the remote
American past. He found *Shadows on the Rock* a pure betrayal, a
symptom of "failure of the will."[19]

Hicks was joined by others—Newton Arvin, John Chamberlain,
Horace Gregory, and Louis Kronenberger among them—men more
likely to admire John Dos Passos' *USA* trilogy or the work of the

young Californian, John Steinbeck. New adjectives entered Cather criticism—*maudlin, feeble, hackneyed*—words as shocking as they were derogatory. Cather's celebrated style itself now became merely one more outward sign of her passivity; and John Chamberlain voiced the prevalent view in five words: "Good prose is not enough." Other mortal flaws were detected. "Her calm pulse," wrote Clifton Fadiman, "did not throb in time with the hurried beat" of the 1920s; and even less was it attuned to the "brutal struggle and mass disaster" of 1932. William Troy, who charged Cather with "facile sentimentalism," asserted that it had been her undoing all along. Newton Arvin proposed that temperament, not critical thought, lay behind her repudiation of Philistine values that, in their fundamentals, "she has never dreamed of challenging."

Lionel Trilling, while retaining more balance than most, felt compelled to assert that the actualities of American life had defeated Willa Cather. Into her use of cliff-dweller jars and Quebec kitchen utensils, readers had read a symbolism of the quest for a high and perfected civilization, but Trilling found something quite the opposite: "if we examine her mystical concern with pots and pans, it does not seem much more than an oblique defense of gentility or very far from the gaudy domesticity of bourgeois accumulation glorified in The Women's Home Companion [sic]. And with it goes a culture-snobbery and even a caste-snobbery."[20]

Hicks, who as usual was willing to go farther, saw in *O Pioneers!* not the triumph of Alexandra Bergson so much as Cather's scorn for the agrarian radicalism of Alexandra's brother; to Hicks, Cather's stance in the novel was symptomatic of a political conservatism that characterized all of her work. At a time when she might have turned to concern for either the present era or the past, she selected the past, with the catastrophic result that she "never once tried to see contemporary life as it is."[21] These were loud voices, but they were in the minority. Willa Cather's books continued to be bought by the public; indeed, *Shadows on the Rock* established itself as a runaway bestseller from the day of its publication. A general reverence for the author continued, and *Time* magazine reflected the predominant opinion that "Willa Cather could not possibly write a bad novel." The question about a forthcoming book was not *whether* but *how* good would be.

V   A Final Estimate

When Willa Cather died in New York City on April 24, 1947, among the many honors she had achieved were the Pulitzer Prize, the Prix Fémina, and the gold medal for fiction awarded by the National Institute of Arts and Letters. In 1934 she was the only American author to have four books shelved in the White House library. Although these honors are nearly meaningless in terms of history, they are an accurate measure of her prestige.

As for what her real contribution to fiction was or is, even now it is too early to say what time will eventually do with Willa Cather. However, the current state of her reputation as a major writer may be gauged by her inclusion in Jackson Bryer's *Sixteen Modern American Authors*. Bryer's selections are based upon queries to 175 students and teachers of American literature, and his question was a simple one: Which Americans should appear in a volume devoted to the most significant writers of the twentieth century? Of all the writers considered—novelists, poets, dramatists—Cather ranked eleventh. Among novelists alone, she ranked seventh; and she is the only woman included in Bryer's volume. To have proved so endurable is no mean feat for a writer dead nearly thirty years; and activity in the world of letters as it observed her centenary indicated that interest in Willa Cather was not diminishing but rather steadily increasing.[22]

In the future critical attention promises to cluster about two apparent centers of interest: Cather as artist and Cather as social critic. Most of the recent attention to Cather has been concerned with her artistry. This focus is only natural when account is taken of the considerable new materials made available by republishing early Cather stories and journalistic pieces. Cather's reputation will probably continue to flow principally from her acknowledged mastery of character, place, and style.

Willa Cather's ability to project human figures of heroic but recognizable stature has explained her appeal for readers since the time of *O Pioneers!* When *The Song of the Lark* appeared and H. W. Boynton declared in print, "These people of Miss Cather's!"[23] he spoke for a majority. And *My Ántonia* prompted the *Daily News* to inform its Chicago audience that, in contrast to the cardboard quality of most fiction purporting to represent the West, no paper dolls were to be found in Cather's work.[24] It seems both inevitable and right that the interest of future readers will continue to be engaged by such dominating figures as Alexandra Bergson, Thea Kronborg, Ántonia Shimerda, Marian Forrester, Godfrey St. Peter, Archbishop Latour, and Anton Rosicky.

The land itself—that considerable southwestern portion of the United States inhabited by the figures just named—unquestionably will more and more be indentifiable as Cather territory. Cather's wish to be delivered from an overly close identification with the West and its cornfields was thwarted even in the one novel that she wrote deliberately to focus upon larger concerns; ironically, reviewers located the high point of *The Professor's House* in the very western materials that she had attempted to minimize. Happily, Cather's fear that attention to locality might doom her to minor literary status has not proven to be true. Her concentration upon the western scene promises to have no long-range negative effect upon her career. On the contrary, Cather's evocation of time and place will surely continue to excite readers, for as time sweeps us further away from the day of the pioneer, we become more alert to its significance. And because, in both surface and spirit, Cather's frontier constitutes an authentic and permanent record of days now extinct, the importance of her role as historian of the American past can be expected to progress unimpeded.

As stylist, Willa Cather has had few peers among American authors. Burton Rascoe's reaction to *Death Comes for the Archbishop*—that the book might be read for the constant enjoyment of its prose alone—seems a bit overstated, even for 1927. Yet its intention remains valid today; for Willa Cather's premeditated effort to refine her language, to purify it, resulted in the creation of an instrument at once subtle, evocative, and flexible; and above all, her method makes for a remarkable clarity of communication. In its simplicity Cather's style is comparable to Ernest Hemingway's, suggesting a common interest in plain English speech, the unadorned phrase; yet Cather's is considerably more deeply rooted in the British tradition, even to its spelling; and both in its vocabulary and in its reliance upon imagery, it has a larger capacity for the poetic. One recalls typical set pieces: the passage from *My Ántonia* in which a plow is silhouetted against the sunset; the descriptions in *Death Comes for the Archbishop* of the New Mexican mesas, each dark bluff topped by its motionless, white cloud-mesa. In these Cather achieves stylistic feats that are not soon forgotten. Like any commanding style, Cather's holds the potential for enhancing her subject materials; and more often than not, that potential is realized.

As a critic of society, Willa Cather has been less well-known than she has in her role as artist. This fact undoubtedly arises from the sharp distinction she made between tracts and novels, on which basis she relegated social issues to subordinate positions in her fiction. The result, as has been noted, was that at moments in her lifetime she could be charged with a lack of concern for contemporary life. That charge never had a firm basis, for Cather's lively attention to both the ideals and the practices of American society is demonstrable at least from the time of "The Sculptor's Funeral," with its satirical thrusts at the religion of practicality and the cult of "getting ahead." In her first novels Willa Cather questioned strongly our enthusiastic national acceptance of money and possession as measures of worth, and she satirized docile veneration of modern products as status symbols. Throughout her career she warned against whatever gained its place at the expense of the human spirit or at the cost of man's healthy relationship with the earth. Most often these warnings were implicit. Cather might isolate an ideal society in time by generations or in space by perching it atop a mesa; yet a contrast of that society with her own epoch always makes itself felt. As an example, in *Death Comes for the Archbishop,* the Indians' way of living in their landscape without disrupting it argues compellingly in favor of ecological balance. Cather typically made her points through such devices rather than by using a more immediate image, say, of a smoky, polluting industrial metropolis of this century (although she could use that urban image also and upon occasion did so with telling effect).[25] The difference is that the portrait of the Indians speaks in hushed tones and works its effects by suggestion. No Jeremiah, Cather by instinct preferred an oblique approach.

On rare occasions, as in *The Professor's House,* Willa Cather did engage in explicit argument. Godfrey St. Peter grapples with a central modern issue when he questions overtly whether science has made human lives better or merely easier. But more characteristically Cather subordinated a message to the human story that always crowds the forefront of her fiction. Even so, it is instructive to recall that long before Sinclair Lewis made a reputation out of the foibles of our dingy but pretentious Main Streets, Willa Cather had already produced a considerable body of "revolt-from-the-village" literature.[26] Because of her artistic convictions Cather could not specialize in photographing the surface of modern life with the completeness of a camera; however, her books have avoided the rapid and injurious dating that has made relics of Lewis' novels, which were such phenomena of popular esteem in their time. Nor could Cather share fully the mechanistic naturalism of her great contemporary, Theodore Dreiser; yet her pessimism about the baleful effects of rampant industrialism on the American landscape and on the national spirit is scarcely less acute than his. In early stories, such as "Paul's Case" and "A Wagner Matinée," which antedate all but the first of Dreiser's tales, Cather gives us characters equally pressed by the weight of circumstance. Cather's people remain much too reserved ever to range the streets of the American city crying *O Lost!* Yet among them are those no less alienated, no less shipwrecked and forlorn, than the behemoths invented by Thomas Wolfe. And while she was under no compulsion to produce a massive trilogy recording the impact of economics and politics on the anonymous generations of this century, Cather's major characters can be fully as shattered by the loss of values as any modern citizens portrayed by John Dos Passos.

The Cather method is at variance with the methods of many writers who created reputations by more directly confronting the immediate moment. Still, her aim is very often the same. At bottom, her concern is with a question critical to our times: to what profit has been our reliance upon science and its technology? That was the question Professor St. Peter raised, of course, and it was the question Cather continued to ask. During the latter stages of World War II, but prior to the dropping of the atomic bomb, Cather foresaw our world brought to the brink of a cataclysm not by any outrageous act of fortune but by the very scientists we thought so clever and intelligent [27] One might legitimately inquire whether since 1945 the human race has proved capable of decelerating its rush toward disaster or whether that tendency has gained momentum politically, economically, and ecologically. The quality of life—what constitutes it, how it can be maintained—is of immediate concern in all of Cather's novels. Thus one looks for her role as social critic to emerge until it assumes its rightful place alongside her role as literary artist.

One doubts that any summary remark can be more pertinent than Henry Seidel Canby's description of Willa Cather's art as being "essentially a representation of the reaction between the soul of man and his environment."[28] Whether she was engrossed with the struggle of young genius to fulfill its felt destiny or with an individual's determination to resist a stultifying social context, this theme was, by and large, her single one. From it and built upon it came the few perfect books that she wanted to leave as her legacy.

Our estimate of Willa Cather has not remained constant, and it is certain to continue to evolve and change; but whatever shifts in judgment the future may bring, in our time many of those for whom literature is a central concern are apparently in substantial agreement with Morton Dauwen Zabel's notion of the Cather significance: "It was her honesty and stubborn sincerity . . . that made possible her real contribution to contemporary literature: she defined, like Dreiser, Scott Fitzgerald, and a few other of her contemporaries between 1910 and 1930, a sense of proportion in American experience. She knew what it meant to be raised in the hinterland of privation and harsh necessities; knew what it meant to look for escape to Chicago and the world beyond; knew how much has to be fought in one's youth and origins, what privileges of the richer world mean when they are approached from the outposts of life, what has to be broken away from and what has to be returned to for later nourishment, and how little the world appears when its romantic distances and remote promise are curtailed to the dimensions of the individual destiny."[29]

Notes and References

Chapter One

1. The role of the railroad in settling Nebraska is portrayed in Richard Overton, *Burlington West* (Cambridge, 1941), and *Burlington Route* (New York, 1965).
2. Overton, *Burlington West*, pp. 334, 352.
3. Material on the Cather family history is contained in a number of sources, including Mildred R. Bennett, *The World of Willa Cather* (New York, 1951); E. K. Brown, *Willa Cather* (New York, 1953); and Edith Lewis, *Willa Cather Living* (New York, 1953).
4. Willa Cather's account of her ride to Catherton is contained in a 1913 interview reprinted in Bernice Slote, *The Kingdom of Art* (Lincoln, 1966), pp. 446–49.
5. Willa Cather, "Nebraska: The End of the First Cycle," *The Nation*, CXVII (September 5, 1923), 237.
6. Slote, p. 449.
7. The report of the Cather auction is as reprinted by the Willa Cather Pioneer Memorial from the Red Cloud *Commercial Advertiser*, September 11, 1884.
8. Bennett, pp. 19–20.
9. *Ibid.*, opp. p. 77, provides a photograph of the Cather-Miner troupe's "Beauty and the Beast" production of 1888.
10. Carrie Miner Sherwood told present writer, 1966.
11. Bennett, pp. 46–47.
12. *Ibid.*, p. 75
13. *Ibid.*, p.113.
14. E. K. Brown and Leon Edel, *Willa Cather* (New York, 1953) pp. 43–46.
15. James R. Shively, ed., *Writings from Willa Cather's Campus Years* (Lincoln, 1950), p. 133.
16. *Ibid.*, p. 128.
17. *Ibid.*, pp. 130, 135.
18. *Ibid.*, p. 139.
19. *Ibid.*, p. 120. The italics are mine.

20. Latrobe Carroll, "Willa Sibert Cather," *Bookman*, LIII (May 1921), 214.

21. These stories are reprinted in Shively, pp. 41–79.

22. Slote, p. 15.

23. *Ibid.*, pp. 267–68.

24. *Ibid.*, pp. 17, 293.

25. *Ibid.*, pp. 122–23, 304.

26. Shively, pp. 37–38.

27. Slote, pp. 380–87.

28. These sentiments were often expressed by Willa Cather in the 1915–1920 era, including an interview in the Omaha *World-Herald*, November 27, 1921, and in Carroll, p. 214.

29. These indentifications are contained in the valuable series of Cather letters to Carrie Miner Sherwood, currently held by the Willa Cather Pioneer Memorial in Red Cloud.

30. In a letter to Carrie Miner Sherwood (October 29, 1917), now in the Alderman Library, Willa Cather says that her portrait of Mrs. Miner in *My Antonia* is realistic enough to be called a snapshot.

31. The most useful record of the way in which Willa Cather drew upon her childhood experiences appears in Bennett, *World of Willa Cather*, which inquires exhaustively into the locales and persons figuring in both Cather's life and fiction.

Chapter Two

1. James Woodress, *Willa Cather* (New York, 1970), p. 72.

2. Slote, *The Kingdom of Art*, pp. 29, 385.

3. Bennett, *Early Stories of Willa Cather* (New York, 1957), p. 110.

4. Elizabeth Moorhead, *These Too Were Here* (Pittsburgh, 1950), p. 47.

5. Willa Cather to Will Owen Jones, September 29, 1900. ALS, Alderman Library.

6. Moorhead, p. 50.

7. *Ibid.*, p. 51.

8. In a letter to Elizabeth Sergeant (August 3, 1916), now in the Alderman Library, Cather predicts that it will always be hard to reconcile herself to the marriage of Isabelle McClung.

9. Brown, *Willa Cather*, p. 103; also George N. Kates, *Willa Cather in Europe* (New York, 1956).

10. *April Twilights* (New York, 1933), p. 25.

11. *Ibid.*, p. 35.

12. Woodress, p. 105.

13. The epigraphs are most thoroughly examined by Slote, pp. 93–97.

14. Carroll, "Willa Sibert Cather," p. 214.

15. Grant Overton, *The Women Who Make Our Novels* (New York, 1918), p. 259.

16. Peter Lyon, *Success Story* (New York, 1963), p. 254.
17. Willa Cather to Will Owen Jones, May 7, 1903. ALS, Alderman Library.
18. *Ibid.*
19. Will Irwin, *The Making of a Reporter* (New York, 1942), pp. 129, 148.
20. Ray Stannard Baker, *American Chronicle* (New York, 1945), p. 95.
21. Lincoln Steffens, *The Autobiography of Lincoln Steffens* (New York, 1945), p. 363.
22. Ida M. Tarbell, *All in the Day's Work* (New York, 1939), p. 199.
23. *Ibid.*, p. 155; also Steffens, pp. 361, 535.
24. Moorhead, p. 52.
25. Lyon, p. 298.
26. *Ibid.*
27. Steffens, p. 364.
28. *Not Under Forty* (New York, 1936), p. 53.
29. *Ibid.*, pp. 60, 71, 75.
30. *Ibid.*, pp. 90, 91.
31. *Ibid.*, p. 95.
32. *Ibid.*, p. 88.
33. *Ibid.*, p. 76.
34. The serialization of McClure's story is accompanied by a reference to Cather's "invaluable assistance," but the book version states: "I am indebted to the cooperation of Miss Willa Sibert Cather for the very existence of this book."
35. Annie Fields, ed., *Letters of Sarah Orne Jewett* (Boston, 1911), p. 249.
36. *Ibid.*, p. 248.
37. *Ibid.*, p. 249.
38. *Ibid.*, p. 247.
39. Between 1910 and 1920, Cather frequently protested the apparent decline in the quality of life in America, particularly in the cities (see: "Behind the Singer Tower," 1912; "Consequences," 1915). During the mid-twenties she was even more fully convinced that the environment had been irrevocably cheapened, and in a letter to Charlotte Stanfield (October 19, 1926), now in the Alderman Library, she complained that New York drove her so to death that she found it imperative to stay away from town for two-thirds of every year. One of the happy things about writing *My Mortal Enemy* was the pleasure she took in recreating the city as it had existed for her earlier in the century, with different—and better—manners.
40. Willa Cather to Elizabeth Sergeant, June 27, 1911. ALS, Alderman Library.
41. "The Bohemian Girl," *McClure's*, XXXIX (August, 1912), 421.
42. Moorhead, p. 54.

43. "Ardessa," *Century*, XCVI (May, 1918), 106.

44. *Ibid.*, p. 107.

45. Cather to Sergeant, April 20, 1912. ALS, Alderman Library.

46. *Ibid.*

47. *Ibid.*

48. *Ibid.* Also: Cather to Sergeant, April 26, 1912. ALS, Alderman Library.

49. Cather to Sergeant, December 7, 1915. ALS, Alderman Library.

50. Cather's letters to Sergeant from the latter part of May through August 1912 are replete with information concerning Julio. See in particular: Cather to Sergeant, May 21, June 15, August 14. ALS, Alderman Library.

51. *The Song of the Lark* (Boston, 1915), pp. 230, 231.

52. Edith Lewis, *Willa Cather Living* (New York, 1953), pp. 93–95.

53. *Ibid.*, pp. 95–99. Also: Cather to Sergeant, August 20, September 21, 1915. ALS, Alderman Library.

54. Lewis, pp. 99–102.

Chapter Three

1. "Training for the Ballet," *McClure's*, XLI (October, 1913), 88.

2. "Three American Singers," *McClure's*, XLII (December, 1913), 33—48.

3. "Plays of Real Life," *McClure's*, XL (March 1913), 25–72.

4. *Ibid.*, p. 72.

5. William M. Curtin, ed., *The World and the Parish* (Lincoln, 1970), II, p. 586.

6. "The Professor's Commencement," *New England Magazine*, XXVI (June, 1902), 487.

7. *One of Ours* (New York, 1922), p. 420.

8. David Daiches, *Willa Cather* (Ithaca, 1951), p. 144.

9. *Youth and the Bright Medusa* (New York, 1920), pp. 66–67.

10. Slote, *The Kingdom of Art*, p. 417.

11. "Plays of Real Life," p. 72.

12. *Youth and the Bright Medusa*, pp. 246–47.

13. *Ibid.*, p. 209.

14. Slote, pp. 408–09.

15. *Alexander's Bridge* (Boston, 1912), p. 144.

16. *Ibid.*, p. 89.

17. Cather to Jones, March 6, 1904; May 29, 1914. TLS. Also: Cather to Sergeant, June 27, 1911. ALS, Alderman Library.

18. Cather to Sergeant, August 10, 1914. ALS, Alderman Library.

19. Willa Cather to Sergeant, n.d., but early February; April 22, 1913. Also: Cather to Zoë Akins, October 31, 1912. ALS, Alderman Library.

20. *O Pioneers!* (Boston, 1913), p. 22.

21. "On the Divide," *Overland Monthly*, XXVII (January, 1896), 67.
22. *O Pioneers!*, p. 64.
23. *Ibid.*, p. 124.
24. "Three American Singers," p. 42.
25. *The Song of the Lark*, Library Edition (Boston, 1937), II, 254.
26. "Plays of Real Life," pp. 68–69.
27. "Three American Singers," p. 48.
28. Cather to Sergeant, April 22, 1913. ALS, Alderman Library.
29. Cather to Sergeant, April 28, 1913; June 23, 1914. ALS, Alderman Library.
30. Cather to Sergeant, June 27, December 7, 1915. ALS, Alderman Library.
31. *Ibid.*, p. 42.
32. *Ibid.*, pp. 42, 48.
33. *Ibid.*, p. 42.
34. Flora Merrill, Interview with Willa Cather in the New York *World*, April 19, 1925, Section 3, p. 6.
35. Cather to Sergeant, April 28, 1913. ALS, Alderman Library.
36. Elizabeth Shepley Sergeant, *Willa Cather: A Memoir* (Lincoln, 1963), p. 139.
37. *My Ántonia* (Boston, 1918), p. xiv.
38. Cather to Jones, May 20, 1919. TLS, Alderman Library.
39. *Ibid.*
40. *My Ántonia*, Library Edition (Boston, 1937), IV, 301.
41. *Ibid.*, p. 123.
42. Eleanor Hinman, Interview with Willa Cather in the Lincoln *Sunday Star*, November 6, 1921.
43. *Ibid.*
44. *My Ántonia*, p. 353.

Chapter Four

1. *One of Ours*, p. 103.
2. Slote, *The Kingdom of Art*, p. 406.
3. "The Professor's Commencement," pp. 481–88.
4. "The Willing Muse," *Century*, LXXIV (August, 1912), 441.
5. "The Enchanted Bluff," *Harper's Monthly Magazine*, CXVIII (April, 1909), 774–81.
6. "The Bohemian Girl," pp. 421–43.
7. "Behind the Singer Tower," *Collier's*, XLVI (May 18, 1912), 16.
8. "Consequences," *McClure's*, XLVI (November, 1915), p. 30.
9. "Her Boss," *Smart Set*, LX (October, 1919), pp. 95–106.
10. *Youth and the Bright Medusa*, p. 138.
11. *Ibid.*, p. 140.

12. *Ibid.*, pp. 268–70.
13. *Ibid.*, p. 226.
14. *O Pioneers!*, p. 172.
15. *The Song of the Lark*, p. 580.
16. "Nebraska: The End of the First Cycle," p. 238.
17. *One of Ours*, p. 18.
18. *Ibid.*, p. 43.
19. *Ibid.*, p. 419.
20. *A Lost Lady* (New York, 1923), pp. 106–07.
21. *Ibid.*, p. 406.
22. *Ibid.*, p. 114.
23. Flora Merrill, Interview, p. 6.
24. *Ibid.*
25. Granville Hicks, "The Case against Willa Cather," in James Schroeter, ed, *Willa Cather and Her Critics* (Ithaca, 1967), pp. 139–47.
26. *The Professor's House* (New York, 1925), pp. 90, 132, 150.
27. *Ibid.*, p. 44.
28. *Ibid.*, p. 69.
29. *Ibid.*, pp. 212–13.
30. *Ibid.*, p. 219.
31. *Ibid.*, p. 221.
32. *Ibid.*, p. 235.
33. *Ibid.*, pp. 244–45.
34. *My Mortal Enemy* (New York, 1926), p. 22.
35. *Ibid.*, p. 40.
36. *Ibid.*, p. 113.
37. *Ibid.*, p. 41.
38. *Ibid.*, p. 104.
39. *Death Comes for the Archbishop* (New York, 1927), pp. 236–37.
40. *Shadows on the Rock* (New York, 1931), p. 25.
41. *Ibid.*, p. 26.
42. *Ibid.*, p. 198.
43. *Ibid.*, p. 98.
44. "Uncle Valentine," *Woman's Home Companion*, LII (February-March 1925), 86.
45. *Ibid.*, p. 80.
46. "Double Birthday," in Edward J. O'Brien, ed., *The Best Short Stories of 1929* (New York, 1929), p. 76.
47. *Ibid.*, p. 83.
48. *Obscure Destinies* (New York, 1932), pp. 30–31.
49. *Ibid.*, pp. 15, 25.
50. *Lucy Gayheart* (New York, 1936), p. 32.
51. *Ibid.*, p. 46.
52. *Ibid.*, p. 112.

53. *Sapphira and the Slave Girl* (New York, 1940), p. 137.
54. *Ibid.*, pp. 210–11.

Chapter Five

1. Slote, *The Kingdom of Art*, p. 258.
2. *Ibid.*, p. 262.
3. *Ibid.*, p. 178.
4. *Ibid.*, pp. 116, 124, 313, 396.
5. *Ibid.*, pp. 119, 152, 161, 339.
6. *Ibid.*, p. 417.
7. *Ibid.*, pp. 142, 161, 226, 407.
8. *Ibid.*, pp. 152, 318; also Curtin, ed., *The World and the Parish*, I, pp. 175, 194.
9. Slote, p. 396.
10. *Ibid.*, p. 311.
11. *Ibid.*, pp. 367, 390; also Curtin, I, p. 79.
12. Slote, p. 178.
13. *Ibid.*, p. 335.
14. *Ibid.*, p. 342.
15. *Ibid.*, pp. 340, 371, 390.
16. *Ibid.*, p. 325.
17. H. W. Boynton, "All Sorts," *Bookman*, XLVIII (December 1918), 495.
18. Edward A. and Lillian D. Bloom, *Willa Cather's Gift of Sympathy* (Carbondale, 1962), p. 246.
19. René Rapin, *Willa Cather* (New York, 1930), p. 98.
20. William H. Nolte, ed., *H. L. Mencken's "Smart Set" Criticism* (Ithaca, 1968), p. 34.
21. Slote, p. 452.
22. Curtin, II, p. 747.
23. *Ibid.*, p. 848.
24. Slote, pp. 351–53.
25. *Ibid.*, p. 332.
26. *Ibid.*, p. 375.
27. *Ibid.*; also Merrill, p. 6.
28. *Slote*, p. 447.
29. Merrill, Interview, p. 6.
30. "Plays of Real Life," p. 72.
31. Fanny Butcher, *Many Lives—One Love* (New York, 1972), p. 366.
32. Carroll, "Willa Sibert Cather," p. 216.

Chapter Six

1. Cather's thirst for acclaim was readily apparent to her childhood

friends and to her college classmates, and in a 1912 letter to Zoë Akins, Cather acknowledged rather frankly her youthful need to glow in the eyes of those she cared about. One of the frustrations of her girlhood, she suggested, was the lack of an appropriate vehicle for making a name for herself. She might have impressed her peers by excelling at horseback riding, perhaps, but in Red Cloud, Nebraska, one stood no hope whatsoever of getting a rise out of a cow by writing a sonnet. Later, of course, as she grew a good deal more sophisticated, and particularly as she realized a few of her personal ambitions and saw her career beginning to blossom, Cather refined her notions of appropriate fame considerably.

2. *Not Under Forty*, pp. 91–92.

3. Curtin, ed., *The World and the Parish*, II, p. 881.

4. Cather to Sergeant, June 2, 1912. ALS, Alderman Library.

5. Butcher, *Many Lives—One Love*, p. 356.

6. Merrill, Interview, p. 6.

7. Slote, *The Kingdom of Art*, p. 387.

8. Curtin, I, p. 58.

9. Nolte, ed., *H. L. Mencken's "Smart Set" Criticism*, p. 263.

10. Frederic Tabor Cooper, "'O Pioneers,'" *Bookman*, XXXVII (August 1913), 667.

11. Frederic Tabor Cooper, "'The Song of the Lark,'" *Bookman*, XLII (November 1915), 323.

12. James Schroeter, ed., *Willa Cather and Her Critics* (Ithaca, 1967), p. 7.

13. H. W. Boynton, "All Sorts," p. 495; also Randolph Bourne, "Morals and Art from the West," *Dial*, LXV (December 14, 1918), 557.

14. Nolte, p. 266.

15. "A Broken Epic," *The Nation*, CXV (October 11, 1922), 388; also Robert Morss Lovett, "Americana," *The New Republic*, XXXII (October 11, 1922), 178.

16. Merrill, p. 6.

17. Jay B. Hubbell, *Who Are the Major American Writers?* (Durham, 1972), pp. 165, 209, 219–21.

18. Robert Cantwell, "A Season's Run," *The New Republic*, LXXXV (December 11, 1935), 149.

19. Granville Hicks, "Bright Incidents," *Forum and Century*, LXXXVI (September 1931), viii; also see Hicks' "The Case Against Willa Cather" in Schroeter, ed., *Willa Cather and Her Critics*, pp. 139–47.

20. Lionel Trilling, "Willa Cather," *The New Republic*, XC (February 10, 1937), 12.

21. Schroeter, p. 144.

22. An analysis of the Bryer poll is contained in Hubbell, pp. 281–84.

23. H. W. Boynton, "Varieties of Realism," *The Nation*, CI (October 14, 1915), 462.

24. Willa Cather reported this to Elizabeth Sergeant, enclosing a copy of an article, "Paper Dolls or People?," which the Chicago *Daily News* had reprinted in its sheet "The Daily News of Business." See: Cather to Sergeant, December 3, 1918. ALS, Alderman Library.

25. See particularly: "The Professor's Commencement" (1902), with its forecast of Pittsburgh as despoiler of the environment.

26. A major theme in Cather's apprentice and early professional writing is the unholiness of the American small town. The theme rises to an eloquent climax in *The Troll Garden* and then continues as Cather turns to the novel. The small towns of *O Pioneers!*, *The Song of the Lark*, *My Ántonia*, and *One of Ours*, with their smug provincialism, bigotry, and narrow-mindedness, are analogues of Lewis' Gopher Prairie.

27. Willa Cather to Viola Roseboro', February 12, 1944. TLS, Alderman Library.

28. Henry Seidel Canby, "Willa Cather (1876–1947)," *The Saturday Review of Literature*, XXX (May 10, 1947), 23.

29. Morton Dauwen Zabel, "Willa Cather," *The Nation*, CLXIV (June 14, 1947), 715.

Selected Bibliography

PRIMARY SOURCES

1. Novels

Alexander's Bridge. Boston: Houghton Mifflin Company, 1912.
Death Comes for the Archbishop. New York: Alfred A. Knopf, 1927.
A Lost Lady. New York: Alfred A. Knopf, 1923.
Lucy Gayheart. New York: Alfred A. Knopf, 1935.
My Ántonia. Boston: Houghton Mifflin Company, 1918.
My Mortal Enemy. New York: Alfred A. Knopf, 1926.
O Pioneers! Boston: Houghton Mifflin Company, 1913.
One of Ours. New York: Alfred A. Knopf, 1922.
The Professor's House. New York: Alfred A. Knopf, 1925.
Sapphira and the Slave Girl. New York: Alfred A. Knopf, 1940.
Shadows on the Rock. New York: Alfred A. Knopf, 1931.
The Song of the Lark. Boston: Houghton Mifflin Company, 1915.

2. Short Story Collections
Obscure Destinies. New York: Alfred A. Knopf, 1932.
The Old Beauty and Others. New York: Alfred A. Knopf, 1948.
The Troll Garden. New York: McClure, Phillips & Co., 1905.
Youth and the Bright Medusa. New York: Alfred A. Knopf, 1920.

3. Poems
April Twilights, Boston: R. G. Badger, 1903.

4. Essay Collections
Not Under Forty. New York: Alfred A. Knopf, 1936.
Willa Cather on Writing. New York: Alfred A. Knopf, 1949.
NOTE: Willa Cather's novels, stories and essays were also published
(1937–41) by Houghton Mifflin Company in a thirteen-volume "Library
Edition."

5. Biography
My Autobiography, New York: Frederick A. Stokes, 1914. Ostensibly by
    S. S. McClure, but actually by Cather.

6. Posthumous Publications

Collected Short Fiction 1892–1912. Ed. by Virginia Faulkner with an introduction by Mildred R. Bennett. Lincoln: University of Nebraska Press, 1970. The most extensive and authoritative collection of Cather's early stories, reprinting works originally published during her college years, her career in Pittsburgh, and her tenure with *McClure's*.

Early Stories of Willa Cather. Selected and with commentary by Mildred Bennett. New York: Dodd, Mead & Company, 1957. Reprints nineteen stories written by Cather between 1892 and 1900 but uncollected by her.

Five Stories. New York: Alfred A. Knopf, 1956. Contains the first reprinting of "The Enchanted Bluff" (1909) as well as an essay by George N. Kates regarding Cather's unfinished Avignon story.

The Kingdom of Art. Ed. by Bernice Slote. Lincoln: University of Nebraska Press, 1966. Cather's dramatic and literary criticism, 1893–96, supplemented by a lengthy and valuable commentary by the editor.

Uncle Valentine and Other Stories. Ed. by Bernice Slote. Lincoln: University of Nebraska Press, 1973. Completes the recovery of Cather's uncollected fiction from 1915 through 1929. Notable for its textual comparison of "Coming, Eden Bower!" and "Coming, Aphrodite!"

Willa Cather in Europe. New York: Alfred A. Knopf, 1956. Reprinting of Cather's journalistic reports from Europe, 1902, with an introduction by George N. Kates.

The World and the Parish. Ed. by William M. Curtin. 2 vol. Lincoln: University of Nebraska Press, 1970. Indispensable collection of Cather's journalism 1893–1902.

Writings from Willa Cather's Campus Years. Ed. by James R. Shively. Lincoln: University of Nebraska Press, 1950. The first reprinting of dramatic criticism and fiction written during 1892–95, a selection accompanied by comments about Cather made by her former college classmates.

SECONDARY SOURCES

1. Biography (books)

BENNETT, MILDRED R. *The World of Willa Cather*. New York: Dodd, Mead & Company, 1951. (Reprinted, Lincoln: University of Nebraska Press, 1961, with notes and index.) A close examination, *in situ*, of the Nebraska background, prepared with the cooperation of many who knew Cather and the models for places or persons in her stories.

BROWN, E. K., and LEON EDEL. *Willa Cather: A Critical Biography*. New York: Alfred A. Knopf, 1953. The most substantial biographical record to date.

BUTCHER, FANNY. *Many Lives—One Love*. New York: Harper & Row, 1972. A chapter is devoted to reminiscences of Cather, whom Butcher knew from 1912 to 1947.

LEWIS, EDITH. *Willa Cather Living*. New York: Alfred A. Knopf, 1953.

Informal biography; important because written by the life-long friend
with whom Cather for many years shared living quarters.

MOORHEAD, ELIZABETH. *These Too Were Here*. Pittsburgh: University of
Pittsburgh Press, 1950. A reminiscence of Louise Homer and Willa
Cather; slight but important for providing data and a viewpoint on the
Pittsburgh years and following.

SERGEANT, ELIZABETH SHEPLEY. *Willa Cather: A Memoir*. Lincoln: University of Nebraska Press, 1963. Reminiscences by a life-long friend;
concerns primarily the years 1910–31.

SLOTE, BERNICE. *Willa Cather: A Pictorial Memoir*. Photographs by Lucia
Woods and others. Lincoln: University of Nebraska Press, 1974. A
comprehensive album of Cather photographs, including many illustra-
tive of her locales and characters.

2.   Criticism (books)

ADAMS, J. DONALD. *The Shape of Books to Come*. New York: The Viking
Press, 1944. Cather approached as an artist of high seriousness; thematic elements seen as more significant than subject matter. Eloquent
defense against Marxist derogation.

AUCHINCLOSS, LOUIS. *Pioneers and Caretakers*. Minneapolis: University of
Minnesota Press, 1965. Astute assessment of Cather's achievement and
career; places *My Mortal Enemy* among her finest work and Sapphira
Colbert among her finest characters. Interesting consideration of
Cather within the context of other twentieth-century women authors.

BEER, THOMAS. "Miss Cather." *The Borzoi, 1925*. New York: Alfred A.
Knopf, 1925. Appreciation of Cather's "art within art"; her achievement of literary tact in an era unnoted for it.

BLOOM, EDWARD A., and LILLIAN D. BLOOM. *Willa Cather's Gift of Sympathy*. Carbondale: Southern Illinois University Press, 1962. Percep-
tive analysis of Cather's themes and techniques; particularly valuable
chapter on the composition of *Death Comes for the Archbishop*.

BOYNTON, PERCY H. *Some Contemporary Americans*. Chicago: University
of Chicago Press, 1924. Chapter devoted to Cather's development as
an artist which finds her in 1924, with *One of Ours* and *A Lost Lady*,
somewhat off her true course.

CONNOLLY, FRANCIS X. "Willa Cather: Memory as Muse." *Fifty Years of
the American Novel*. Ed. by Harold C. Gardiner, S. J. New York:
Charles Scribner's Sons, 1951. Interesting readings of *My Ántonia*, *The
Professor's House*, and *Death Comes for the Archbishop*, considered
Cather's crucial novels in terms of her "passion for order" and the
limitations it imposed upon her work.

DAICHES, DAVID. *Willa Cather: A Critical Introduction*. Ithaca: Cornell
University Press, 1951. Reading of the novels and stories; assessment
of Cather's position in American literature; important for the attention
paid to her style.

GEISMAR, MAXWELL. *The Last of the Provincials*. Boston: Houghton Mifflin Company, 1947. General appraisal of Cather in her times; centers on the "cultural wound" caused by the dominance of an emerging industrialism whose implications Cather reflects in her work but never directly portrayed. Unusual in considering *Lucy Gayheart* among the most convincing of the novels.

GIANNONE, RICHARD. *Music in Willa Cather's Fiction*. Lincoln: University of Nebraska Press, 1966. Specialized, persuasive study of the centrality of music in Cather's stories and its influence upon theme, character, and form.

HARTWICK, HARRY. *The Foreground of American Fiction*. New York: American Book Company, 1934. Estimate of Cather's position in literary history; emphasizes her differences from the naturalists.

HOFFMAN, FREDERICK J. *The Twenties*. Rev. ed. New York: The Free Press, 1962. Presents *The Professor's House* as a key novel in depicting the clash between the modern and the traditional during the 1920s.

JONES, HOWARD MUMFORD. *The Bright Medusa*. Urbana: University of Illinois Press, 1952. Denies Cather withdrew from life; instead, says she lived it on another plane; praises development of character and sense of life's dignity.

KAZIN, ALFRED. *On Native Grounds*. New York: Reynall and Hitchcock, 1942. Presents Cather as elegist for a lost world of tradition that she sees as grander than its modern substitute.

MENCKEN, H. L. "Willa Cather." *The Borzoi, 1920*. New York: Alfred A. Knopf, 1920. Brief essay; announces arrival of Cather as a mature, major writer; of interest because of its timing and because it summarizes the opinions of an early Cather admirer.

MURPHY, JOHN J., ed. *Five Essays on Willa Cather*. North Andover, Mass: Merrimack College, 1974. The proceedings of the Cather symposium held at Merrimack in 1972. Offers a valuable updated bibliography of biographical and critical sources.

RANDALL, JOHN H., III. *The Landscape and the Looking Glass*. Boston: Houghton Mifflin Company, 1960. Penetrating analysis of Cather's novels, centers on her search for value and balances her strengths and weaknesses as a novelist. A major study.

RANDALL, JOHN H., III. "Willa Cather and the Decline of Greatness." *The Twenties: Poetry and Prose*. Ed. by Richard E. Langford and William E. Taylor. Deland, Florida: Everett Edwards Press, Inc., 1966. Cather's alienation from modern American society as indicated in her novels of the 1920s; traces her growing pessimism regarding the possibility of a life devoted to the fine and the beautiful.

RAPIN, RENÉ. *Willa Cather*. New York: Robert M. McBride & Company, 1930. First critical volume devoted to Cather; particularly interesting because of the time in which it appeared and because of its indepen-

dent judgments, such as *One of Ours* being among Cather's finest
work; *A Lost Lady*, among her minor.

SCHROETER, JAMES, ed. *Willa Cather and Her Critics*. Ithaca: Cornell
University Press, 1967. To date, the only collection of critical pieces by
various authors that covers a spectrum from 1916 to 1965. Highly
useful, even though not definitive.

SERGEANT, ELIZABETH SHEPLEY. *Fire Under the Andes*. New York: Alfred
A. Knopf, 1927. Essay on Cather; traces development of her reputation; links her works closely to her biography.

SHERMAN, STUART. *Critical Woodcuts*. New York: Charles Scribner's Sons,
1926. Chapter on Willa Cather; sees effort of the individual to live out
his potentialities as vital center of her novels.

SLOTE, BERNICE. "Willa Cather." *Sixteen Modern American Authors*, ed.
by Jackson Bryer. Durham: Duke University Press, 1974. Long essay;
the most comprehensive survey of Cather criticism available. Considers all aspects.

SLOTE, BERNICE, and VIRGINIA FAULKNER, eds. *The Art of Willa Cather*.
Lincoln: University of Nebraska Press, 1974. Proceedings of the international seminar held in observation of the Cather centennial in October 1973 in Lincoln.

VAN GHENT, DOROTHY. *Willa Cather*. Minneapolis: University of Minnesota Press, 1964. A pamphlet-length essay spanning the breadth of
Cather's accomplishment economically and perceptively; emphasizes
her search for self and security.

WOODRESS, JAMES. *Willa Cather: Her Life and Art*. New York: Western
Publishing Co., 1970. The most recent of full-length studies and one of
the finest; scholarly but highly readable; making use of new materials,
including letters. Independent in making judgments.

3.   Criticism (periodicals)

Pieces contained in Schroeter (see sections above) generally will not be
cited here.

BENNETT, MILDRED R. "How Willa Cather Chose Her Names," *Names*, X
(March 1962) 29–37. Interesting example of Mrs. Bennett's investigations into Nebraska source materials for Cather's novels.

BAUM, BERNARD. "Willa Cather's Waste Land," *The South Atlantic Quarterly*, XLVIII (October 1949), 589–601. Persuasive essay; links Cather
with the generalized "waste land" spirit of the 1920s; allies her thematically with Eliot, Fitzgerald, Ransom, MacLeish, Tate, and others.
Points to striking parallels between Eliot's poem and her novels.

FADIMAN, CLIFTON. "Willa Cather: The Past Recaptured," *The Nation*,
CXXXV (December 7, 1932), 563–65. Typical assessment of the 1930s,
in which Cather's "hypertrophied" sense of the past is seen as a threat
to her position as a major artist.

FEGER, LOIS. "The Dark Dimension of Willa Cather's *My Ántonia*," *The*

English Journal, LXIX (September 1970), 774–79. Representative of latter-day critical interests; analyzes novel for pattern of images utilizing danger, coldness, and the dark to balance the "happy" theme of the book.

FOOTMAN, ROBERT H. "The Genius of Willa Cather," *American Literature*, X (May 1938), 123–41. Uses Cather's limitations (here, her economic, religious and esthetic motivations) as a means of defining her genius. Important article.

GELFANT, BLANCHE H. "The Forgotton Reaping-Hook: Sex in *My Ántonia*," *American Literature*, XL (March 1971), 60–82. Concentrates on Jim Burden, his disguised sexual fears and regressive tendencies, and the theme of narcissism.

GERBER, PHILIP L. "Willa Cather and the Big Red Rock," *College English*, XIX (January 1958), 152–57. Examines the thematic implications of the rock symbol as it appears in Cather's stories and novels from "The Enchanted Bluff" (1909) to *Shadows on the Rock* (1931).

HINZ, JOHN. "*A Lost Lady* and *The Professor's House*," *The Virginia Quarterly Review*, XXIX (Winter 1953), 70–85. Original analysis of *The Professor's House* in the context of its times and of Cather's life. Links novel with the early story "The Professor's Commencement" (1902).

JONES, HOWARD MUMFORD. "The Novels of Willa Cather," *The Saturday Review of Literature*, XVIII (August 6, 1938), 3–4, 16. Assessment of Cather's contribution made after the publication of the Library Edition; balanced appraisal but defense of Cather's noninterest in men and women as economic creatures.

KRONENBERGER, LOUIS. "Willa Cather," *Bookman*, LXXIV (October 1931), 134–40. Appraises Cather as the most human and solid of contemporary novelists; sees her moving in the wrong direction with *Shadows on the Rock*.

MARTIN, TERENCE. "The Drama of Memory in *My Ántonia*," *PMLA*, LXXXIV (March 1969), 304–11. Places emphasis upon Jim Burden who, as narrator, reveals his own story and the reasons why Ántonia epitomizes human values for him.

MORRIS, LLOYD. "Willa Cather," *North American Review*, CCXIX (April 1924), 641–52. Important early assessment of Cather's work, its strength and weaknesses; sees her as celebrant of a lost tradition that has no adequate modern parallel.

WINSTEN, ARCHER. "A Defense of Willa Cather," *Bookman*, LXXIV (March 1932), 634–40. Defends Cather against the Marxist attacks then beginning.

Index

180